PRAXIS

PRINCIPLES OF LEARNING AND TEACHING (7-12) 0524

By: Sharon Wynne, M.S.

XAMonline, INC.
Boston

To obtain permission(s) to use the material from this work for any purpose including workshops or seminars, please submit a written request to:

XAMonline, Inc.
25 First Street, Suite 106
Cambridge, MA 02141
Toll Free 1-800-509-4128
Email: info@xamonline.com
Web: www.xamonline.com
Fax: 1-617-583-5552

Library of Congress Cataloging-in-Publication Data

Wynne, Sharon A.
    PRAXIS Principles of Learning and Teaching (7-126) 0524 / Sharon A. Wynne. 1st ed
    ISBN 978-1-60787-027-2
    1. Principles of Learning and Teaching (7-12) 0524
    2. Study Guides
    3. PRAXIS
    4. Teachers' Certification & Licensure
    5. Careers

Disclaimer:

The opinions expressed in this publication are the sole works of XAMonline and were created independently from the National Education Association, Educational Testing Service, or any State Department of Education, National Evaluation Systems or other testing affiliates.

Between the time of publication and printing, state specific standards as well as testing formats and Web site information may change and therefore would not be included in part or in whole within this product. Sample test questions are developed by XAMonline and reflect content similar to that on real tests; however, they are not former test questions. XAMonline assembles content that aligns with state standards but makes no claims nor guarantees teacher candidates a passing score. Numerical scores are determined by testing companies such as NES or ETS and then are compared with individual state standards. A passing score varies from state to state.

Printed in the United States of America   œ-1

PRAXIS Principles of Learning and Teaching (7-12) 0524
ISBN: 978-1-60787-027-2

Table of Contents

PRAXIS

PRINCIPLES OF LEARNING AND TEACHING (7-12) 0524

SECTION 1
ABOUT XAMONLINE

XAMonline—A Specialty Teacher Certification Company

Created in 1996, XAMonline was the first company to publish study guides for state-specific teacher certification examinations. Founder Sharon Wynne found it frustrating that materials were not available for teacher certification preparation and decided to create the first single, state-specific guide. XAMonline has grown into a company of over 1,800 contributors and writers and offers over 300 titles for the entire PRAXIS series and every state examination. No matter what state you plan on teaching in, XAMonline has a unique teacher certification study guide just for you.

XAMonline—Value and Innovation

We are committed to providing value and innovation. Our print-on-demand technology allows us to be the first in the market to reflect changes in test standards and user feedback as they occur. Our guides are written by experienced teachers who are experts in their fields. And our content reflects the highest standards of quality. Comprehensive practice tests with varied levels of rigor means that your study experience will closely match the actual in-test experience.

To date, XAMonline has helped nearly 600,000 teachers pass their certification or licensing exams. Our commitment to preparation exceeds simply providing the proper material for study—it extends to helping teachers **gain mastery** of the subject matter, giving them the **tools** to become the most effective classroom leaders possible, and ushering today's students toward a **successful future**.

SECTION 2
ABOUT THIS STUDY GUIDE

Purpose of This Guide

Is there a little voice inside of you saying, "Am I ready?" Our goal is to replace that little voice and remove all doubt with a new voice that says, "I AM READY. **Bring it on!**" by offering the highest quality of teacher certification study guides.

Organization of Content

You will see that while every test may start with overlapping general topics, each is very unique in the skills they wish to test. Only XAMonline presents custom content that analyzes deeper than a title, a subarea, or an objective. Only XAMonline presents content and sample test assessments along with **focus statements**, the deepest-level rationale and interpretation of the skills that are unique to the exam.

Title and field number of test

→Each exam has its own name and number. XAMonline's guides are written to give you the content you need to know for the specific exam you are taking. You can be confident when you buy our guide that it contains the information you need to study for the specific test you are taking.

Subareas

→These are the major content categories found on the exam. XAMonline's guides are written to cover all of the subareas found in the test frameworks developed for the exam.

Objectives

→These are standards that are unique to the exam and represent the main subcategories of the subareas/content categories. XAMonline's guides are written to address every specific objective required to pass the exam.

Focus statements

→These are examples and interpretations of the objectives. You find them in parenthesis directly following the objective. They provide detailed examples of the range, type, and level of content that appear on the test questions. **Only XAMonline's guides drill down to this level.**

How Do We Compare with Our Competitors?

XAMonline—drills down to the focus statement level.
CliffsNotes and REA—organized at the objective level
Kaplan—provides only links to content
MoMedia—content not specific to the state test

Each subarea is divided into manageable sections that cover the specific skill areas. Explanations are easy to understand and thorough. You'll find that every test answer contains a rejoinder so if you need a refresher or further review after taking the test, you'll know exactly to which section you must return.

How to Use This Book

Our informal polls show that most people begin studying up to eight weeks prior to the test date, so start early. Then ask yourself some questions: How much do you really know? Are you coming to the test straight from your teacher-education program or are you having to review subjects you haven't considered in ten years? Either way, take a **diagnostic or assessment test** first. Also, spend time on sample tests so that you become accustomed to the way the actual test will appear.

This guide comes with an online diagnostic test of 30 questions found online at *www.XAMonline.com*. It is a little boot camp to get you up for the task and reveal things about your compendium of knowledge in general. Although this guide is structured to follow the order of the test, you are not required to study in that order. By finding a time-management and study plan that fits your life you will be more effective. The results of your diagnostic or self-assessment test can be a guide for how to manage your time and point you toward an area that needs more attention.

After taking the diagnostic exam, fill out the **Personalized Study Plan** page at the beginning of each chapter. Review the competencies and skills covered in that chapter and check the boxes that apply to your study needs. If there are sections you already know you can skip, check the "skip it" box. Taking this step will give you a study plan for each chapter.

Week	Activity
8 weeks prior to test	Take a diagnostic test found at www.XAMonline.com
7 weeks prior to test	Build your Personalized Study Plan for each chapter. Check the "skip it" box for sections you feel you are already strong in. ✗ SKIP IT ☐
6-3 weeks prior to test	For each of these four weeks, choose a content area to study. You don't have to go in the order of the book. It may be that you start with the content that needs the most review. Alternately, you may want to ease yourself into plan by starting with the most familiar material.
2 weeks prior to test	Take the sample test, score it, and create a review plan for the final week before the test.
1 week prior to test	Following your plan (which will likely be aligned with the areas that need the most review) go back and study the sections that align with the questions you may have gotten wrong. Then go back and study the sections related to the questions you answered correctly. If need be, create flashcards and drill yourself on any area that you makes you anxious.

SECTION 3
ABOUT THE PRAXIS EXAMS

What Is PRAXIS?

PRAXIS II tests measure the knowledge of specific content areas in K-12 education. The test is a way of insuring that educators are prepared to not only teach in a particular subject area, but also have the necessary teaching skills to be effective. The Educational Testing Service administers the test in most states and has worked with the states to develop the material so that it is appropriate for state standards.

PRAXIS Points

1. The PRAXIS Series comprises more than 140 different tests in over seventy different subject areas.

2. Over 90% of the PRAXIS tests measure subject area knowledge.

3. The purpose of the test is to measure whether the teacher candidate possesses a sufficient level of knowledge and skills to perform job duties effectively and responsibly.

4. Your state sets the acceptable passing score.

5. Any candidate, whether from a traditional teaching-preparation path or an alternative route, can seek to enter the teaching profession by taking a PRAXIS test.

6. PRAXIS tests are updated regularly to ensure current content.

Often **your own state's requirements** determine whether or not you should take any particular test. The most reliable source of information regarding this is either your state's Department of Education or the Educational Testing Service. Either resource should also have a complete list of testing centers and dates. Test dates vary by subject area and not all test dates necessarily include your particular test, so be sure to check carefully.

If you are in a teacher-education program, check with the Education Department or the Certification Officer for specific information for testing and testing timelines. The Certification Office should have most of the information you need.

If you choose an alternative route to certification you can either rely on our Web site at *www.XAMonline.com* or on the resources provided by an alternative certification program. Many states now have specific agencies devoted to alternative certification and there are some national organizations as well:

National Center for Education Information
http://www.ncei.com/Alt-Teacher-Cert.htm

National Associate for Alternative Certification
http://www.alt-teachercert.org/index.asp

Interpreting Test Results

Contrary to what you may have heard, the results of a PRAXIS test are not based on time. More accurately, you will be scored on the raw number of points you earn in relation to the raw number of points available. Each question is worth one raw point. It is likely to your benefit to complete as many questions in the time allotted, but it will not necessarily work to your advantage if you hurry through the test.

Follow the guidelines provided by ETS for interpreting your score. The web site offers a sample test score sheet and clearly explains how the scores are scaled and what to expect if you have an essay portion on your test.

Scores are usually available by phone within a month of the test date and scores will be sent to your chosen institution(s) within six weeks. Additionally, ETS now makes online, downloadable reports available for 45 days from the reporting date.

It is **critical** that you are aware of your own state's passing score. Your raw score may qualify you to teach in some states, but not all. ETS administers the test and assigns a score, but the states make their own interpretations and, in some cases, consider combined scores if you are testing in more than one area.

What's on the Test?

PRAXIS tests vary from subject to subject and sometimes even within subject area. For PRAXIS Principles of Learning and Teaching 7-12 (0524), the test lasts for 2 hours and consists of approximately 12 short-answer questions and 24 multiple-choice questions. The 12 short-answer questions take the format of 4 case studies, each of which will be followed by 3 short-answer questions. The 24 multiple-choice questions are presented in two separate sections of 12 questions each. The breakdown of the questions is as follows:

Category	Question Format	Approximate Percentage of the test	Suggested Time to Spend on this Section
I: Students as Learners	Multiple-choice	11%	6-7 minutes

Table continued on next page

Category	Question Format	Approximate Percentage of the test	Suggested Time to Spend on this Section
II: Instruction and Assessment	Multiple-choice	11%	6-7 minutes
III: Teacher Professionalism	Multiple-choice	11%	6-7 minutes
IV: Students as Learners	Short answer	22%	25 minutes
V: Instruction and Assessment	Short answer	22%	25 minutes
VI: Communication Techniques	Short answer	11%	25 minutes
VII: Teacher Professionalism	Short answer	11%	25 minutes

Question Types

You're probably thinking, enough already, I want to study! Indulge us a little longer while we explain that there is actually more than one type of multiple-choice question. You can thank us later after you realize how well prepared you are for your exam.

1. Complete the Statement. The name says it all. In this question type you'll be asked to choose the correct completion of a given statement. For example:

> **The Dolch Basic Sight Words consist of a relatively short list of words that children should be able to:**
>
> A. Sound out
>
> B. Know the meaning of
>
> C. Recognize on sight
>
> D. Use in a sentence

The correct answer is A. In order to check your answer, test out the statement by adding the choices to the end of it.

2. **Which of the Following.** One way to test your answer choice for this type of question is to replace the phrase "which of the following" with your selection. Use this example:

> **Which of the following words is one of the twelve most frequently used in children's reading texts:**
>
> A. There
>
> B. This
>
> C. The
>
> D. An

Don't look! Test your answer. _____ is one of the twelve most frequently used in children's reading texts. Did you guess C? Then you guessed correctly.

3. **Roman Numeral Choices.** This question type is used when there is more than one possible correct answer. For example:

> **Which of the following two arguments accurately supports the use of cooperative learning as an effective method of instruction?**
> I.   Cooperative learning groups facilitate healthy competition between individuals in the group.
> II.   Cooperative learning groups allow academic achievers to carry or cover for academic underachievers.
> III. Cooperative learning groups make each student in the group accountable for the success of the group.
> IV.   Cooperative learning groups make it possible for students to reward other group members for achieving.
>
> A. I and II
>
> B. II and III
>
> C. I and III
>
> D. III and IV

Notice that the question states there are **two** possible answers. It's best to read all the possibilities first before looking at the answer choices. In this case, the correct answer is D.

4. **Negative Questions.** This type of question contains words such as "not," "least," and "except." Each correct answer will be the statement that does **not** fit the situation described in the question. Such as:

> **Multicultural education is not**
>
> A. An idea or concept
>
> B. A "tack-on" to the school curriculum
>
> C. An educational reform movement
>
> D. A process

Think to yourself that the statement could be anything but the correct answer. This question form is more open to interpretation than other types, so read carefully and don't forget that you're answering a negative statement.

5. **Questions that Include Graphs, Tables, or Reading Passages.** As always, read the question carefully. It likely asks for a very specific answer and not a broad interpretation of the visual. Here is a simple (though not statistically accurate) example of a graph question:

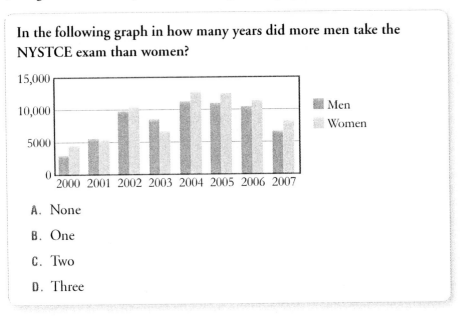

> **In the following graph in how many years did more men take the NYSTCE exam than women?**
>
> A. None
>
> B. One
>
> C. Two
>
> D. Three

It may help you to simply circle the two years that answer the question. Make sure you've read the question thoroughly and once you've made your determination, double check your work. The correct answer is C.

SECTION 4
HELPFUL HINTS

Study Tips

1. **You are what you eat.** Certain foods aid the learning process by releasing natural memory enhancers called CCKs (cholecystokinin) composed of tryptophan, choline, and phenylalanine. All of these chemicals enhance the neurotransmitters associated with memory and certain foods release memory enhancing chemicals. A light meal or snacks of one of the following foods fall into this category:

   - Milk
   - Rice
   - Eggs
   - Fish
   - Nuts and seeds
   - Oats
   - Turkey

   The better the connections, the more you comprehend!

2. **See the forest for the trees.** In other words, get the concept before you look at the details. One way to do this is to take notes as you read, paraphrasing or summarizing in your own words. Putting the concept in terms that are comfortable and familiar may increase retention.

3. **Question authority.** Ask why, why, why? Pull apart written material paragraph by paragraph and don't forget the captions under the illustrations. For example, if a heading reads *Stream Erosion* put it in the form of a question (Why do streams erode? What is stream erosion?) then find the answer within the material. If you train your mind to think in this manner you will learn more and prepare yourself for answering test questions.

4. **Play mind games.** Using your brain for reading or puzzles keeps it flexible. Even with a limited amount of time your brain can take in data (much like a computer) and store it for later use. In ten minutes you can: read two paragraphs (at least), quiz yourself with flash cards, or review notes. Even if you don't fully understand something on the first pass, your mind stores it for recall, which is why frequent reading or review increases chances of retention and comprehension.

5. **The pen is mightier than the sword.** Learn to take great notes. A by-product of our modern culture is that we have grown accustomed to getting our information in short doses. We've subconsciously trained ourselves to assimilate information into neat little packages. Messy notes fragment the flow of information. Your notes can be much clearer with proper formatting. *The Cornell Method* is one such format. This method was popularized in *How to Study in College*, Ninth Edition, by Walter Pauk. You can benefit from the method without purchasing an additional book by simply looking up the method online. Below is a sample of how *The Cornell Method* can be adapted for use with this guide.

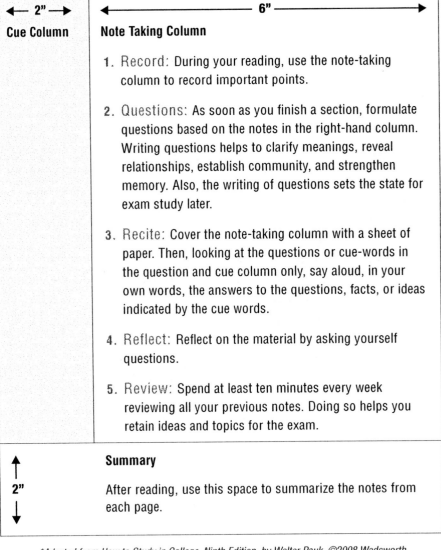

← 2" →	← 6" →
Cue Column	**Note Taking Column**
	1. Record: During your reading, use the note-taking column to record important points.
	2. Questions: As soon as you finish a section, formulate questions based on the notes in the right-hand column. Writing questions helps to clarify meanings, reveal relationships, establish community, and strengthen memory. Also, the writing of questions sets the state for exam study later.
	3. Recite: Cover the note-taking column with a sheet of paper. Then, looking at the questions or cue-words in the question and cue column only, say aloud, in your own words, the answers to the questions, facts, or ideas indicated by the cue words.
	4. Reflect: Reflect on the material by asking yourself questions.
	5. Review: Spend at least ten minutes every week reviewing all your previous notes. Doing so helps you retain ideas and topics for the exam.
↑ 2" ↓	**Summary** After reading, use this space to summarize the notes from each page.

*Adapted from How to Study in College, Ninth Edition, by Walter Pauk, ©2008 Wadsworth

6. **Place yourself in exile and set the mood.** Set aside a particular place and time to study that best suits your personal needs and biorhythms. If you're a night person, burn the midnight oil. If you're a morning person set yourself up with some coffee and get to it. Make your study time and place as free from distraction as possible and surround yourself with what you need, be it silence or music. Studies have shown that music can aid in concentration, absorption, and retrieval of information. Not all music, though. Classical music is said to work best

7. **Get pointed in the right direction.** Use arrows to point to important passages or pieces of information. It's easier to read than a page full of yellow highlights. Highlighting can be used sparingly, but add an arrow to the margin to call attention to it.

8. **Check your budget.** You should at least review all the content material before your test, but allocate the most amount of time to the areas that need the most refreshing. It sounds obvious, but it's easy to forget. You can use the study rubric above to balance your study budget.

The proctor will write the start time where it can be seen and then, later, provide the time remaining, typically fifteen minutes before the end of the test.

Testing Tips

1. **Get smart, play dumb.** Sometimes a question is just a question. No one is out to trick you, so don't assume that the test writer is looking for something other than what was asked. Stick to the question as written and don't overanalyze.

2. **Do a double take.** Read test questions and answer choices at least twice because it's easy to miss something, to transpose a word or some letters. If you have no idea what the correct answer is, skip it and come back later if there's time. If you're still clueless, it's okay to guess. Remember, you're scored on the number of questions you answer correctly and you're not penalized for wrong answers. The worst case scenario is that you miss a point from a good guess.

3. **Turn it on its ear.** The syntax of a question can often provide a clue, so make things interesting and turn the question into a statement to see if it changes the meaning or relates better (or worse) to the answer choices.

4. **Get out your magnifying glass.** Look for hidden clues in the questions because it's difficult to write a multiple-choice question without giving away part of the answer in the options presented. In most questions you can readily eliminate one or two potential answers, increasing your chances of answering correctly to 50/50, which will help out if you've skipped a question and gone back to it (see tip #2).

5. **Call it intuition.** Often your first instinct is correct. If you've been studying the content you've likely absorbed something and have subconsciously retained the knowledge. On questions you're not sure about trust your instincts because a first impression is usually correct.

6. **Graffiti.** Sometimes it's a good idea to mark your answers directly on the test booklet and go back to fill in the optical scan sheet later. You don't get extra points for perfectly blackened ovals. If you choose to manage your test this way, be sure not to mismark your answers when you transcribe to the scan sheet.

7. **Become a clock-watcher.** You have a set amount of time to answer the questions. Don't get bogged down laboring over a question you're not sure about when there are ten others you could answer more readily. If you choose to follow the advice of tip #6, be sure you leave time near the end to go back and fill in the scan sheet.

Do the Drill

No matter how prepared you feel it's sometimes a good idea to apply Murphy's Law. So the following tips might seem silly, mundane, or obvious, but we're including them anyway.

1. **Remember, you are what you eat, so bring a snack.** Choose from the list of energizing foods that appear earlier in the introduction.

2. **You're not too sexy for your test.** Wear comfortable clothes. You'll be distracted if your belt is too tight or if you're too cold or too hot.

3. **Lie to yourself.** Even if you think you're a prompt person, pretend you're not and leave plenty of time to get to the testing center. Map it out ahead of time and do a dry run if you have to. There's no need to add road rage to your list of anxieties.

4. **Bring sharp number 2 pencils.** It may seem impossible to forget this need from your school days, but you might. And make sure the erasers are intact, too.

5. **No ticket, no test.** Bring your admission ticket as well as **two** forms of identification, including one with a picture and signature. You will not be admitted to the test without these things.

6. **You can't take it with you.** Leave any study aids, dictionaries, notebooks, computers, and the like at home. Certain tests **do** allow a scientific or four-function calculator, so check ahead of time to see if your test does.

7. **Prepare for the desert.** Any time spent on a bathroom break **cannot** be made up later, so use your judgment on the amount you eat or drink.

8. **Quiet, Please!** Keeping your own time is a good idea, but not with a timepiece that has a loud ticker. If you use a watch, take it off and place it nearby but not so that it distracts you. And **silence your cell phone**.

To the best of our ability, we have compiled the content you need to know in this book and in the accompanying online resources. The rest is up to you. You can use the study and testing tips or you can follow your own methods. Either way, you can be confident that there aren't any missing pieces of information and there shouldn't be any surprises in the content on the test.

If you have questions about test fees, registration, electronic testing, or other content verification issues please visit *www.ets.org*.

Good luck!

Sharon Wynne
Founder, XAMonline

DOMAIN I
STUDENTS AS LEARNERS

PERSONALIZED STUDY PLAN

✗
KNOWN
MATERIAL/
SKIP IT

COMPETENCY 1
STUDENT DEVELOPMENT AND
THE LEARNING PROCESS

> **SKILL 1.1** Knows theoretical knowledge about how learning occurs, how students construct knowledge, and how students develop habits of mind

Today, teachers are immediately faced with the challenge of deciding whether they believe that the classroom should be teacher-centered or student-centered. Usually, an appropriate combination of both is preferred; thus, most teachers must negotiate which areas of their instruction should be teacher-centered and which areas should be student-centered.

Classroom Styles

TEACHER-CENTERED CLASSROOMS generally focus on the concept that knowledge is objective and that students must learn new information through the transmission of that knowledge from the teacher. STUDENT-CENTERED CLASSROOMS are considered to be constructivist, in that students are given opportunities to construct their own meanings onto new pieces of knowledge. Doing so may require that students are more actively involved in the learning process. Indeed, constructivism is a strong force in teaching today, but it is often misinterpreted. Good constructivist teachers do NOT just let their students explore anything they want in any way they choose; rather, they give students opportunities to learn things in more natural ways, such as through experiments, hands-on projects, discussions, etc.

Constructivist theory

The most current theory of constructivist learning allows students to construct learning opportunities. For constructivist teachers, the belief is that students create their own reality of knowledge and how to process and observe the world around them. Students are constantly constructing new ideas, which serve as frameworks for learning and teaching. Researchers have shown that the constructivist model is composed of four components:

TEACHER-CENTERED CLASSROOMS: classrooms that focus on the concept that knowledge is objective and that students must learn new information through the transmission of that knowledge from the teacher

STUDENT-CENTERED CLASSROOMS: classrooms in which students are given opportunities to construct their own meanings onto new pieces of knowledge; these classrooms are considered constructivist

CONSTRUCTIVIST LEARNING
Learner creates knowledge
Learner constructs and makes meaningful new knowledge to existing knowledge
Learner shapes and constructs knowledge by life experiences and social interactions
In constructivist learning communities, the student, teacher and classmates establish knowledge cooperatively on a daily basis

According to Kelly (1969), "human beings construct knowledge systems based on their observations"; this statement parallels Jean Piaget's theory that knowledge is constructed as individuals work with others who have similar background and thought processes. Constructivist learning for students is dynamic and ongoing. For constructivist teachers, the classroom becomes a place where students are supported and encouraged to interact with the instructional process by asking questions and applying new ideas to old theories.

Learning Theories

A classic learning theorist, Piaget believed students passed through a series of stages to develop from the most basic forms of concrete thinking to sophisticated levels of abstract thinking. His developmental theory consists of four learning stages, which can be remembered with the following mnemonic, Stages Precious Children Follow (SPCF):

1. Sensory motor stage (from birth to age two)

2. Preoperation stage (ages two to seven or early elementary)

3. Concrete operational (ages seven to eleven or upper elementary)

4. Formal operational (ages seven to fifteen or late elementary/high school)

Additional prominent learning theories in education today include brain-based learning and the Multiple Intelligence Theory. Supported by recent brain research, brain-based learning suggests that knowledge about the way the brain retains information enables educators to design the most effective learning environments. As a result, researchers have developed twelve principles that relate knowledge about the brain to teaching practices.

The twelve principles of brain-based learning:

- *The brain is a complex adaptive system*
- *The brain is social*
- *The search for meaning is innate*
- *We use patterns to learn more effectively*
- *Emotions are crucial to developing patterns*
- *Each brain perceives and creates parts and whole simultaneously*
- *Learning involves focused and peripheral attention*
- *Learning involves conscious and unconscious processes*
- *We have at least two ways of organizing memory*
- *Learning is developmental*
- *Complex learning is enhanced by challenge (and inhibited by threat)*
- *Every brain is unique*

Caine & Caine, 1994, Mind/Brain Learning Principles

To maximize student learning, educators can use these principles to help design methods and environments in their classrooms.

Sample Test Questions and Rationale

(Easy)

1. Constructivist classrooms are considered to be:

   A. Student-centered

   B. Teacher-centered

   C. Focused on standardized tests

   D. Requiring little creativity

   The answer is A.

   Student-centered classrooms are considered to be "constructivist," in that students are given opportunities to construct their own meanings onto new pieces of knowledge.

(Average)

2. Which of the following is not a stage in Piaget's theory of child development?

   A. Sensory motor stage

   B. Preoptimal stage

   C. Concrete operational

   D. Formal operational

   The answer is B.

   Jean Piaget believed students passed through a series of stages to develop from the most basic forms of concrete thinking to sophisticated levels of abstract thinking. His developmental theory consists of four learning stages, which can be remembered with the following pneumonic, Stages Precious Children Follow (SPCF):

   1. Sensory motor stage (from birth to age 2)

   2. Preoperation stage (ages 2 to 7 or early elementary)

   3. Concrete operational (ages 7 to 11 or upper elementary)

   4. Formal operational (ages 7 to 15 or late elementary/high school)

SKILL 1.2 Knows human development in the physical, social, emotional, moral, speech/language, and cognitive domains

To be successful, a teacher must have a broad knowledge and thorough understanding of the development that typically occurs during the students' current period of life. More importantly, the teacher understands how students learn best during each period of development. The most important premise of student development is that all domains of development (physical, social, and academic) are integrated. Development in each dimension is influenced by the other dimensions. Moreover, today's educator must also have knowledge of exceptionalities and how these exceptionalities affect all domains of a student's development.

Physical Development

It is important for the teacher to be aware of the physical stage of development and how the student's physical growth and development affect the student's cognitive learning. Factors determined by the physical stage of development include: ability to sit and attend, the need for activity, the relationship between physical skills and self-esteem, and the degree to which physical involvement in an activity (as opposed to being able to understand an abstract concept) affects learning.

Cognitive (Academic) Development

Students go through patterns of learning, beginning with preoperational thought processes, and they move to concrete operational thoughts. Eventually they begin to acquire the mental ability to think about and solve problems in their head because they can manipulate objects symbolically. Students of most ages can use symbols such as words and numbers to represent objects and relations, but they need concrete reference points. To facilitate cognitive development, it is essential that students be encouraged to use and develop the thinking skills that they possess in solving problems that interest them. The content of the curriculum must be relevant, engaging, and meaningful to the students.

Social Development

Students progress through a variety of social stages. First, they begin with an awareness of their peers but have a lack of concern for the presence of these other children. Young children engage in "parallel" activities playing alongside their peers without directly interacting with one another. Next, during the primary years, children develop an intense interest in peers. They establish productive, positive social and working relationships with one another. This stage of social growth continues throughout the child's formative period including the primary, middle, and high school years. It is necessary for teachers to recognize the importance of developing positive peer-group relationships and to provide opportunities and support for cooperative small group projects that not only develop cognitive ability but also promote peer interaction. The ability to work and relate effectively with peers is of major importance and contributes greatly to the child's sense of competence. In order to develop this sense of competence, children need to be successful in acquiring the knowledge and skills recognized by their culture as important; in the United States, among the most important are those skills that promote academic achievement.

Developmental Orientation

DEVELOPMENTALLY ORIENTED TEACHERS: teachers that approach classroom groups and individual students with a respect for their emerging capabilities

Knowledge of age-appropriate expectations is fundamental to both the teacher's positive relationship with students and his or her ability to develop effective instructional strategies. Equally important is the knowledge of what is appropriate for individual students in a classroom. **DEVELOPMENTALLY ORIENTED TEACHERS** approach classroom groups and individual students with a respect for their emerging capabilities. Developmentalists recognize that kids grow in common patterns but at different rates, which usually cannot be accelerated by adult pressure or input. These teachers also know that variations in the school performance of different students often results from differences in their general growth. Most school districts use inclusion to ensure that all students receive a free and appropriate education. Therefore, it is vital for teachers to know the characteristics of students' exceptionalities and their implications for learning.

The effective teacher is cognizant of students' individual learning styles, human growth, and development theories, and how to apply these principles in the selection and implementation of appropriate instructional activities.

COMPETENCY 2
STUDENTS AS DIVERSE LEARNERS

SKILL 2.1 **Knows differences in the ways students learn and perform**

Selection of Learning Activities

The effective teacher is cognizant of students' individual learning styles, human growth, and development theories, and how to apply these principles in the selection and implementation of appropriate instructional activities. Learning activities selected for early childhood (below age eight) should occur in short time frames in highly simplified form. The nature of the activity and the context in which the activity is presented affects the approach that the students will take in processing the information. During early childhood, children tend to process information at a slower rate than when they are older (age eight and beyond).

Selecting activities

When selecting and implementing learning activities for older students, teachers should focus on more complex instructional activities for which these students are developmentally prepared. Moreover, effective teachers maintain a clear understanding of the developmental appropriateness of activities selected. They also present these activities in a manner consistent with the level of readiness of their students.

Different Learning Theories

For quite some time, a movement called "multiple intelligences" has been popular in many classrooms. The MULTIPLE INTELLIGENCE THEORY, developed by Howard Gardner, suggests that students learn in (at least) seven different ways. It also proposes that verbal/linguistic and quantitative intelligences, the two types that are most often associated with intellect, should be reconsidered to be as (not more) important compared to the other forms of intelligence. Other intelligences included kinesthetic, interpersonal, musical, intrapersonal, and spatial. This theory has helped teachers understand that while some students may not excel in one style of learning, it is entirely possible that they are incredibly gifted in another.

Academic subject areas have also added to the philosophical debate on teaching. For example, reading teachers have long debated whether phonics or whole language was more appropriate as an instructional method. Language Arts teachers have debated the importance of a prescribed canon (famous works of literature) versus teaching literature simply to teach thinking skills and an appreciation of good literature. Math teachers have debated the extent to which application is necessary in math instruction; while some feel that it is more important to teach structure and process, others suggest that it is only relevant if math skills are taught in context.

Cognitive theory

Researchers Joyce and Weil (1996) described THE THEORY OF METACOGNITION as first the study of how to help the learner gain understanding about how knowledge is constructed; and second arming that learner with the conscious tools for constructing that knowledge. The COGNITIVE APPROACH to learning emphasizes that the teacher must understand that the greatest learning and retention opportunities in the classroom come from teaching the student to process his or her own

MULTIPLE INTELLIGENCE THEORY: a theory that states that students learn in at least seven different ways, including verbal/linguistic, quantitative, interpersonal, musical, intrapersonal, and spatial

THE THEORY OF METACOGNITION: the study of how to help the learner gain understanding about how knowledge is constructed

COGNITIVE APPROACH: the study of, first, how to help the learner gain understanding about how knowledge is constructed, and second, arming that learner with the conscious tools for constructing that knowledge

learning to master the skill being taught. Students are taught to develop concepts and teach themselves skills in problem solving and critical thinking. The student becomes the active participant in the learning process and the teacher becomes the facilitator of that conceptual and cognitive learning process.

Social and behavioral theories

Social and behavioral theories look at how students' social interactions instruct or impact learning opportunities in the classroom. Both theories are subject to individual variables that are learned and applied either positively or negatively in the classroom. Innumerable stimuli in the classroom can promote learning or evoke behavior that is counterproductive for both students and teachers. As human beings, students are social and normally gravitate to action in the classroom; therefore, to maximize learning opportunities, teachers must be deliberate in planning classroom environments that provide both focus and engagement

Designing a classroom

Designing classrooms that provide optimal academic and behavioral support for diverse students can be daunting for teachers. The ultimate goal is creating a safe learning environment where students can construct knowledge in an engaging and positive climate.

No one of these theories will work for every classroom, and a good approach is to incorporate a range of learning theories in a classroom. Still, under the guidance of any theory, good educators will differentiate their instructional practices to meet the needs of individual students' abilities and interests using various instructional practices.

Sample Test Questions and Rationale

(Rigorous)

1. Mr. Rogers describes his educational philosophy as eclectic, meaning that he uses many educational theories to guide his classroom practice. Why is this the best approach for today's teachers?

    A. Today's classrooms are often too diverse for one theory to meet the needs of all students

    B. Educators must be able to draw upon other strategies if one theory is not effective

    C. Both A and B

    D. None of the above

    The answer is C.

    No one theory will work for every classroom; a good approach is for an educator to incorporate a range of learning theories in his or her practice. Still, under the guidance of any theory, good educators will differentiate their instructional practices to meet the needs of individual students' abilities and interests using various instructional practices.

(Rigorous)

2. Which of the following statements MOST explain how philosophy has impacted other subject areas such as reading, math, and science?

    A. Most subject areas emerged from Greek society and its great philosophers such as Plato and Aristotle

    B. Using philosophical arguments, experts have debated the best teaching strategies in various subject areas

    C. Philosophy drives the motivation and dedication of most great teachers

    D. A majority of the fifty states require students to take several years of philosophical courses

    The answer is B.

    Academic subject areas have also added to the philosophical debate on teaching. For example, reading teachers have long debated whether phonics or whole language was more appropriate as an instructional method. Language Arts teachers have debated the importance of a prescribed canon (famous works of literature) versus teaching literature simply to teach thinking skills and an appreciation of good literature. Math teachers have debated the extent to which application is necessary in math instruction; while some feel that it is more important to teach structure and process, others suggest that it is only relevant if math skills are taught in context.

Sample Test Questions and Rationale (cont.)

(Average)

3. You notice that one of your students is having a seizure and classmates inform you that this is because she was abusing drugs at her locker. What should you do immediately after contacting the main office about this emergency?

   A. Attempt to treat the student

   B. Find out the protocol for your school district

   C. Isolate the student until EMS or police arrive

   D. Interview classmates individually to gather the facts

The answer is C.

Never, under any circumstances, attempt to treat, protect, tolerate, or negotiate with a student who is showing signs of a physical crisis. It is advisable to find out the protocol for a particular school or district; however, most schools require the student to be isolated until they are removed from the school center by EMS or police.

SKILL 2.2 Knows areas of exceptionality in students' learning

In student learning, there are many areas of exceptionalities. These areas can include students who are challenged, talented and gifted (TAG), and/or emotionally stressed or abused.

Students with Learning Disabilities

Teachers must be able to identify students with disabilities while maintaining their right to privacy. Often, students and their parents may be aware of a particular disability; however, they will not want peers or even teachers to know. Some disabilities necessitate special school care or medical attention by nurses or counseling staff. In these cases, administrators and teachers are often notified. Again, confidentiality and caution must be maintained.

There is significant disagreement over the term "disability," itself. Many people argue that it suggests a defect in a person's character. While disabilities can be physical, there are also learning disabilities, which can be related to an individual's ability to learn or communicate.

The term "students with disabilities" is quite broad; thus, there are few common characteristics among students with disabilities. In a generic sense, most disabilities hamper an individual's development or his or her ability to perform specific actions. For example, any degree of deafness will negatively affect auditory development; people with multiple sclerosis may have trouble with muscle function; and those who have Attention Deficit Hyperactivity Disorder (ADHD) may have trouble with concentration. It is important to remember that students with disabilities in one (or multiple) area(s) can still be highly functioning in other domains. In fact, even students with specific disabilities may not have all the possible challenges of that particular disability.

The term "students with disabilities" is quite broad; thus, there are few common characteristics among students with disabilities. In a generic sense, most disabilities hamper an individual's development or his/her ability to perform specific actions.

Addressing disabled students' needs

Some disabilities may be obvious, particularly those that are physical. In such cases physical or behavioral abnormalities may be noticed by teachers and peers. Therefore, teachers must notice, correct, and reduce or eliminate teasing or bullying.

An **INDIVIDUAL EDUCATION PLAN (IEP)** provides an academic framework for a student with a disability. The IEP is developed by a team of educational professionals and is a tool by which teachers can ensure that a student diagnosed with a particular disability can maximize his or her potential.

INDIVIDUAL EDUCATION PLAN (IEP): a plan that provides an academic framework for a student with a disability

Educators have become increasingly alert for and attentive to students with learning disabilities. These may include auditory or visual processing disabilities, attention deficit hyperactivity disorder, autism, and others. While educators and researchers are sensitive to all disabilities, the field has seen autism skyrocket among young children. This condition usually presents itself within the first three years of a child's life and hinders normal communication and social interactive behavior; it is thought to be a lifetime condition.

See Skill 2.3 for more information on referring and helping students with disabilities.

Emotional Stress and Abuse

Because all students experience stressful periods within their lives from time to time, all students may demonstrate some behaviors that indicate emotional distress. Emotionally healthy students can maintain control of their own behavior even during stressful times. The difference between typical stress-response behavior and severe emotional distress is determined by the frequency, duration, and intensity of stress-responsive behavior.

Signs of emotional distress

Lying, stealing, and fighting are maladaptive behaviors that any student may exhibit occasionally; however, if a student lies, steals, or fights regularly or blatantly, then these behaviors may be indicative of emotional distress. Lying can be especially common among young children who do so to avoid punishment or as a means to make themselves feel more important. But as they move out of early childhood, lying can be a signal that students are feeling insecure. If feelings of insecurity escalate, lying may become habitual or obvious and that may indicate that the student is seeking attention because of emotional distress. Fighting, especially among siblings, is a common occurrence. However, if a student fights constantly, is unduly aggressive, or is belligerent toward others on a long-term basis, teachers and parents need to consider the possibility of emotional problems.

It is imperative that teachers are able to identify when children need help with their behavior, therefore, educators must constantly monitor student behaviors; it is through actions that children will indicate that they need and/or want help. Repeatedly breaking established rules or destroying property can signify that a student is losing control. Other signs that a child needs help may include frequent bouts of crying, a quarrelsome attitude, and constant complaints about school, friends, or life in general. Any time a child's disposition, attitude, or habits change significantly, teachers and parents must seriously consider emotional difficulties.

It is imperative that teachers are able to identify when children need help with their behavior, therefore, educators must constantly monitor student behaviors; it is through actions that children will indicate that they need and/or want help.

Addressing emotionally distressed students

Classroom teachers have many safe and helpful interventions to assist them with students who are suffering serious emotional disturbances. First, the teacher must communicate the nature and extent of the suspected issues. Next, the school involves other professionals and parents/guardians in order to provide an appropriate safety net for the intervention. This is done unless the parents/guardians are suspected as the source of abuse. Finally, two-way communication constantly flows between the home and school, on a daily basis if necessary, to ensure that the student has a successful transition back to appropriate thoughts and behaviors.

By establishing environments that promote appropriate behavior for all students, teachers can reduce negative behaviors in the classroom. First, clear rules must be established and should include the understanding that students are to have respect for one another. If necessary, classmates may need to be informed of a students' special needs so they can give due consideration. For instance, if a student is blind, the teacher will need to explain the disability and specify that students keep the room in order at all times so that their classmate can navigate.

Behavior modification programs

For any student who might show emotional or behavioral disorders, a BEHAVIOR MODIFICATION PROGRAM is usually effective. Severe disorders may require that on a regular basis a school psychologist, guidance counselor, or behavior specialist is directly involved with the student and provides counseling and therapy. Frequently such interventions also involve the student's family. If deviant behavior does occur, the teacher should have a plan of action to difuse the situation and protect the student and other individuals. Such a plan could include a safe and secure time-out place where the student can go to regain self-control.

> **BEHAVIOR MODIFICATION PROGRAM:** a course of action designed to help a student deal with emotional or behavioral disorders

Neurotic Disorders

Emotional disorders can escalate so severely that the student's well-being is threatened. Teachers and parents must recognize the signs of severe emotional stress, which may become detrimental to the student and others. During child-hood, of the various forms of emotional disorders, neurotic disorders are the second most common group. Physical symptoms of NEUROSES include:

- Extreme or ongoing anxiety
- Overdependence
- Social isolation
- Sleep problems
- Nausea
- Abdominal pain
- Diarrhea
- Headaches

> **NEUROSIS:** a psychological disorder that is characterized by general distress

Students may also have irrational fears of particular objects or situations or become consumed with obsessions, thoughts, or ideas. One of the most serious neuroses is depression. Signs that a child is depressed include:

- Ongoing sadness
- Crying
- Lack of interest in people or activities
- Eating and sleep disorders
- Talking about wanting to be dead

Teachers and other adults must listen to what the student is saying and should take these verbal expressions very seriously. Many schoolhouse tragedies, including

Columbine, CO, Jonesboro, AR, and Lake Worth, FL, may have been prevented if the signs of emotional issues had been recognized and resolved.

Psychotic Disorders

PSYCHOSIS:
a psychological disorder that is characterized by a loss of contact with reality

Even more serious than neurosis is PSYCHOSIS, which is characterized by a loss of contact with reality. Psychosis is rare in childhood, but when it does occur, it is often difficult to diagnose. One fairly constant sign is failure to make normal emotional contact with other people. With schizophrenia, a common psychosis of childhood, the individual deliberately escapes from reality and withdraws from relationships with others. This disorder can be described as a person having contact with others, but through a curtain. Schizophrenia is more common in boys than in girls, and a major sign is a habitually flat or habitually agitated facial expression. Students suffering from schizophrenia are occasionally mute, but at times they talk incessantly using bizarre words in ways that make no sense. In a vicious cycle, their incoherent speech contributes to their frustration, and this compounds their fears and preoccupation.

Early Infantile Autism

EARLY INFANTILE AUTISM: a disorder that is characterized by impaired social interaction and communication

The cause of EARLY INFANTILE AUTISM is unknown. In the past, some psychiatrists speculated that these children did not develop normally due to a lack of parental warmth. This has been dismissed as unlikely because the incidence of autism in families is usually limited to one child. While there are no scientific confirmations, some theorize that the disorder may be caused by metabolic or chromosomal defects.

Signs of early infantile autism

Early infantile autism may occur as early as the fourth month of life and may present itself as an infant lying apathetically and oblivious in the crib. In other cases, the baby appears to develop at a normal pace throughout infancy only to have the symptoms appear without warning at about eighteen months of age. Due to the nature of the symptoms, autistic children are often misdiagnosed as mentally retarded, deaf-mute, or organically brain-damaged. With this disorder as well, boys are twice as likely as girls to be diagnosed.

According to many psychologists who have been involved with treating autistic children, it seems that these children have built a wall between themselves and everyone else, including their families, and even their parents. They do not make eye contact with others and do not even appear to hear the voices of those who speak to them. They cannot empathize with others and have no ability to appreciate humor.

Autistic children usually have language disturbances. One third never develop any speech; however, they may grunt or whine. Others may repeat the same word or phrase over and over or "parrot" what someone else has said. They often lack inner-language and cannot play by themselves above a primitive, sensory-motor level.

Frequently, autistic children will develop a preoccupation with objects; this appears to fill the void left by the absence of interpersonal relationships. They become compulsive about the arrangements of objects and often engage in simple, repetitive physical activities with objects for long periods of time. If these activities are interrupted, they may react with fear or rage. Others remain motionless for hours each day sometimes moving only their eyes or hands.

Socialization of autistic children

The developmental abilities of autistic students varies greatly. On intelligence tests they may score from severely subnormal to high average. Some exhibit astonishing abilities in isolated skill areas; for instance, one student may memorize volumes of material, another could sing beautifully, and a third could perform complicated mathematical problems. This phenomenon was popularized by the movie *Rainman*.

The prognosis for autistic children is painfully discouraging. Only about five percent of autistic children become socially well adjusted in adulthood. Another twenty percent make fair social adjustments. The remaining seventy-five percent are socially incapacitated and must be supervised for the duration of their lives.

Treatment may include outpatient psychotherapy, drugs, or long-term treatment in a residential center; however, for the long term, neither the presence nor absence of treatment appears to make a difference.

Behaviors Indicating Drug/Alcohol Abuse

Legally, the use of any illicit substance by a minor, including alcohol, is automatically considered abuse. This issue must be tackled by educators because illegal substances hamper and reduce social and academic functioning. The adage "Pot makes a smart kid average and an average kid dumb" is quite accurate with almost every controlled substance. There exist not a few families where substance abuse, such as pot smoking, is a known habit of the parents. Parental use hampers national drug and alcohol prevention efforts because students may start their dependency by stealing from parents. In addition, parental use negates the message that substance abuse is wrong.

WITHDRAWAL: a stage of substance abuse when substance is removed from the blood stream and a metabolic craving is accompanied by sweating, nausea, dizziness, elevated blood pressure, seizures, and, in rare instances, death

BLACKOUT: a stage of substance abuse when a dependent experiences serious physical symptoms but later doesn't remember anything of his or her actions

In the school setting, hard signs of dependency are rare and when seen, they must be considered very serious.

TOLERANCE: the final stage of substance abuse characterized by a resistance to the effects of the substance; this changes over the course of the disease, increasing in the early stages and decreasing in the late chronic stage

Stages of substance abuse

Substance abuse, regardless of the substance, follows a pattern of withdrawal, blackouts, and tolerance. WITHDRAWAL occurs when the substance is removed from the blood stream and a metabolic craving is accompanied by:

- Sweating
- Nausea
- Dizziness
- Elevated blood pressure
- Seizures
- Death (in rare instances)

During the BLACKOUT stage a dependent experiences serious physical symptoms but later doesn't remember anything of his or her actions. The anesthetized mind has eliminated conscious wakeful activity, functioning mainly on instinct. TOLERANCE is the final stage and changes over the course of the disease, increasing in the early stages and decreasing in the late chronic stage.

Dangers of unaddressed substance abuse

In the school setting, hard signs of dependency are rare and when seen, they must be considered very serious. Due to the danger of long-term injury or fatality, substance ingestion must be treated immediately by medical staff. Fatalities can occur in cases of seizures due to withdrawal, overdoses due to mixed substances, or overuse of a single substance including overdoses with alcohol alone. Never, under any circumstances, attempt to treat, protect, tolerate, or negotiate with a student who is showing signs of a physical crisis. It is advisable to find out the protocol for a particular school or district; however, most schools require the student to be isolated until they are removed from the school center by EMS or police.

Abuse vs. dependency

While there is a difference between abuse and dependency, for this age group they can be viewed in the same light. This is particularly true because for young people, addiction occurs at a high rate, rapidly after first use, and sometimes after only a few tries. Abuse is a lesser degree of involvement with substances; usually implying the person is not physically addicted. They may have just as many "soft signs" of involvement but lack true addiction. Dependency indicates a true physical addiction, characterized by several hard signs, some of which are less likely to be seen in a school setting. When deprived of the substance, the person may experience withdrawal symptoms, blackouts, tolerance, irresponsibility, and illogical behavior. Soft signs include declines in functioning in all domains including social and occupational, mental and emotional, and spiritual life.

Social signs of substance abuse

Social decline is one of the signs of drug or alcohol abuse. In being acquainted with all students, educators will notice personality changes in any student. Characteristically, social withdrawal is first noticed when the student fails to say hello, avoids being near teachers, seems evasive or sneaky, and associates with a different, less academically focused, group of friends. Obviously, association with known substance abusers is almost always a warning sign. Adults must not accept the explanation that the suspected abuser is just being friends with the known abuser, or that the suspected abuser has other kinds of friends. There is a sharp demarcation between youth who abuse substances and those who do not. Typically, a young person does not straddle the line unless they intend to "hop the fence" once in a while.

The abuser will progressively disregard their appearance, showing up unclean, unkempt, and disheveled. Actual style of fashion may change to more radical trends such as nose rings, body piercings, and tattoos. Such fashion choices are used by nonabusing youth and, on their own, are not an indication of substance abuse; however, there does seem to be a high correlation. The socially impaired substance abuser will frequently be late for school, classes, and other appointments. The abuser seeks less and less satisfaction from traditional social activities such as school athletics, rallies, plays, student government, and after-school programs. In contrast, some abusers hide behind conformity, going to great pains to appear normal; these may be some of the most seriously impaired of all.

> There is a sharp demarcation between youth who abuse substances and those who do not. Typically, a young person does not straddle the line unless they intend to "hop the fence" once in a while.

Mental/emotional signs of substance abuse

Mental and emotional impairments manifest as the addiction deepens. Academic indicators include declining school performance, standardized test scores, and interest in school. In addition, students with addictions may:

- Respond more slowly to prompts, sharp noises, or sudden actions

- Show emotional flattening and personality changes

- Have vacant expressions, hyperactivity, depression, psychosis, and a lack of motivation

- Discuss or attempt suicide

Students already having emotional problems (about three to six percent of any given population of youth) are more vulnerable to using drugs and alcohol than students who are well adjusted. Caution is recommended when educators question teenagers to ascertain drug and alcohol abuse. Students might have another psychiatric illness of which the school is not aware. They may appear to be high or intoxicated; but instead, they may be reacting to medications. Their odd behavior may be due to the psychiatric illness itself, not substance abuse. Thus, whenever possible, it is helpful to know a student's history.

Spiritual signs of substance abuse

The last step is spiritual decline, an even less obvious manifestation than the other signs of substance abuse. The broadest definition of SPIRITUALITY is the youth's existential relationship to the greater world around him or her. Attitudes of respect, humility, wonder, and affection indicate a person who has a sense of relationship to something greater. Attitudes of contempt, pride, ignorance, and arrogance indicate one who lacks an awareness of the enormity of existence. More specifically, a previously religious or reverent student may suddenly become blatantly disrespectful of organized religion. The inappropriate use of the cross or other religious symbol may also indicate spiritual decline.

> **SPIRITUALITY:** the youth's existential relationship to the greater world around him or her

Reasons for substance abuse

Although most students understand the dangers of drug and alcohol use, hardcore users cannot resist involvement. They may disregard the dangers because their emotional pain is so high. In today's complex world, many factors lead to high levels of emotional pain, not the least of which is family and community breakdown. Today, the divorce rate is extremely high and approximately one half of families are blended. Students are transported from parent to parent, often against their own wishes, and ex-spouses may retaliate against each other through children. Students from these families feel guilt, anger, and shame, feelings that can be dangerous as they usually remain unresolved. Once considered relatively harmless to children, divorce is now being reevaluated and is now viewed as a serious challenge.

Other causes of emotional pain to students include:

- Social awkwardness
- Depression
- Undiagnosed and/or untreated mental illnesses
- Personality disorders
- Learning disabilities
- ADHD

- Conduct disorders

- Substance abuse and dependency in family members

The most common manifestation of emotional pain are parent–child issues, which include deficits in communication, authority, and respect between parent(s) and student(s). An equally common signal of emotional issues is conduct disorders, a behavior set characterized by:

- Aggression

- Exploitation

- Violence

- Disregard for the rights of others

- Animal cruelty

- Fire-setting

- Bed-wetting

- Defiance

- Running away

- Truancy

- Juvenile arrest records

- ADHD

- Substance abuse

Sample Test Questions and Rationale

(Average)

1. This condition has skyrocketed among young children, usually presents itself within the first three years of a child's life, and hinders normal communication and social interactive behavior.

   A. ADHD

   B. Dyslexia

   C. Depression

   D. Autism

The answer is D.

Educators and researchers are sensitive to all disabilities; however, the field has seen autism skyrocket among young children. This condition usually presents itself within the first three years of a child's life and hinders normal communication and social interactive behavior.

(Average)

2. The difference between typical stress-response behavior and severe emotional distress can be identified by the:

   A. Situation, circumstances, and individuals around which the behavior occurs

   B. The family dynamics of the student

   C. Frequency, duration, and intensity of the stress-responsive behavior

   D. The student's age, maturity, and coping abilities

The answer is A.

Because all students experience stressful periods within their lives from time to time, all students may demonstrate some behaviors that indicate emotional distress. Emotionally healthy students can maintain control of their own behavior even during stressful times. The difference between typical stress-response behavior and severe emotional distress is determined by the frequency, duration, and intensity of stress-responsive behavior.

Sample Test Questions and Rationale (cont.)

(Easy)

3. **It is essential that teachers develop relationships with their students and are aware of their personalities. Which of the following is an example of why this is important?**

   A. Because most students do not have adult friends

   B. Because most teachers do not have friends who are students

   C. So that teachers can stay abreast of the social interaction between students

   D. Because then teachers can immediately identify behavioral changes and get the student help

The answer is D.

Social decline is one of the signs of drug or alcohol abuse. Being acquainted with all students, educators will notice personality changes in any student. Characteristically, social withdrawal is first noticed when the student fails to say hello, avoids being near teachers, seems evasive or sneaky, and associates with a different, less academically focused, group of friends. Obviously, association with known substance abusers is almost always a warning sign. Adults must not accept the explanation that the suspected abuser is just being friends with the known abuser, or that the suspected abuser has many kinds of friends. There is a sharp demarcation between youth who abuse substances and those who do not.

SKILL 2.3 Knows legislation and institutional responsibilities relating to exceptional students

History of Disabilities Legislation

The U.S. Constitution does not specify protection for education. However, all states provide education, and thus individuals are guaranteed protection and due process under the 14th Amendment. The basic source of law for special education is the **INDIVIDUALS WITH DISABILITIES EDUCATION ACT (IDEA)** and its accompanying regulations. IDEA represents the latest phase in the philosophy of educating students with disabilities. Initially, students with disabilities often did not go to

INDIVIDUALS WITH DISABILITIES EDUCATION ACT (IDEA): the basic source of law for special education; the latest phase in the philosophy of educating studetns with disabilities

school. When they did, they were segregated into special classes in order to avoid disrupting the regular class. Their education usually consisted of simple academics and later, training for manual jobs.

By the mid-1900s, advocates for students with special needs argued that segregation was inherently unequal. By the time of P.L. 94-142, about half of the estimated 8 million students with special needs in the U.S. were either not being appropriately served in school or were excluded from schooling altogether. There was a disproportionate number of minority students placed in special programs. Identification and placement practices and procedures were inconsistent, and parental involvement was generally not encouraged. After segregation on the basis of race was declared unconstitutional in BROWN V. BOARD OF EDUCATION, parents and other advocates filed similar lawsuits on behalf of students with special needs. The culmination of their efforts resulted in P.L. 94-142. This section is a brief summary of that law and other major legislation, which affect the manner in which special education services are delivered to students in need of those services.

> **BROWN V. BOARD OF EDUCATION:** the court decision that determined that the segregation on the basis of race was declared unconstitutional

IDEA P.L. 101-476 (1990)

The principles of IDEA also incorporate the concept of "normalization." Within this concept, persons with disabilities are allowed access to everyday patterns and conditions of life that are as close as possible or equal to their nondisabled peers. There are seven fundamental provisions of IDEA.

1. Free Appropriate Public Education (FAPE): Special Education services are to be provided at no cost to students or their families. The federal and state governments share any additional costs. FAPE also requires that education be appropriate to the individual needs of the students.

2. Notification and procedural rights for parents. These include:
   - The right to examine records and obtain independent evaluations.
   - The right to receive a clearly written notice that states the results of the school's evaluation of their student and whether the student meets eligibility requirements for placement or continuation of special services.
   - The right for parents who disagree with the school's decision to request a due process hearing and a judicial hearing if they do not receive satisfaction through due process.

3. Identification and services to all students: States must conduct public outreach programs to seek out and identify students who may need services.

4. Necessary related services: Developmental, corrective, and other support services that make it possible for a student to benefit from special

education services must be provided. These may include speech, recreation, or physical therapy.

5. Individualized assessments: Evaluations and tests must be nondiscriminatory and individualized.

6. Individualized Education Plans: Each student receiving special education services must have an individualized education plan developed at a meeting that is attended by a qualified representative of the local education agency (LEA). Others who should attend would be the proposed special education teachers, mainstream teachers, parents, and, when appropriate, the student.

7. Least restrictive Environment (LRE): There is no simple definition of LRE. LRE differs with the student's needs. LRE means that the student is placed in an environment, which is not dangerous or overly controlling or intrusive. The student should be given opportunities to experience what other peers of similar mental or chronological age are doing. Finally, LRE should be the environment that is the most integrated and normalized for the student's strengths and weaknesses. LRE for one child may be a regular classroom with support services, while LRE for another may be a self-contained classroom in a special school.

Individuals with Disabilities Act and Child Study Teams

Collaborative teams play a crucial role in meeting the needs of all students, and they are important in identifying students with special needs. Under IDEA, it is the responsibility of public schools to ensure consultative, evaluative, and if necessary, prescriptive services to students with special needs. In most school districts, this responsibility is handled by a collaborative group called the CHILD STUDY TEAM (CST). If a teacher or parent suspects a student to have academic, social, or emotional problems the student is referred to the CST where a team consisting of educational professionals (including teachers, specialists, the school psychologist, guidance, and other support staff) review the student's case and situation through meetings with the teacher and/or parents/guardians. The CST will determine what evaluations or tests are necessary. They will also assess the results and suggest a plan of action if one is necessary.

Intervention plans

One plan of action is an ACADEMIC INTERVENTION PLAN (AIP). An AIP consists of additional instructional services that are provided to the student in order to help him or her better achieve academically. Another plan of action is a 504 PLAN. This is a legal document based on the provisions of the Rehabilitation Act of 1973

Under IDEA, it is the responsibility of public schools to ensure consultative, evaluative, and, if necessary, prescriptive services to students with special needs. In most school districts, this responsibility is handled by a collaborative group called the Child Study Team (CST).

CHILD STUDY TEAM (CST): a collaborative group that ensures consultative, evaluative, and, if necessary, prescriptive services to students with special needs

ACADEMIC INTERVENTION PLAN (AIP): an action plan consisting of additional instructional services that are provided to the student in order to help them better achieve academically

504 PLAN: a plan that provides instructional services to assist students with special needs in a regular-education classroom setting

(which preceded IDEA). A 504 plan provides instructional services to assist students with special needs in a regular-education classroom setting. Typically, the CST and perhaps even the student's physician or therapist will participate in the 504 meeting and review to determine if a 504 plan will be written.

Finally, a student referred to the CST may qualify for an **INDIVIDUALIZED EDUCATION PLAN (IEP)**. An IEP is a legal document that delineates the specific adaptive services a student will receive. An IEP differs from a 504 plan in that the child must be identified for special education services to qualify for an IEP, and all students who receive special education services must have an IEP. Each IEP must contain statements pertaining to the student's:

> **INDIVIDUALIZED EDUCATION PLAN (IEP):** a legal document that delineates the specific adaptive services a student will receive

- Present performance level
- Annual goals
- Related services
- Supplementary aids
- Testing modifications
- A projected date of services
- Assessment methods for monitoring progress

Each year, the CST and parent/guardians must meet to review and update a student's IEP.

Family Involvement

Under the IDEA, parent/guardian involvement in the development of the student's IEP is required and absolutely essential for the advocacy of the student's educational needs. IEPs must be tailored to meet the student's needs, and no one knows those needs better than the parent/guardian and other significant family members. Optimal conditions for a disabled student's education exist when teachers, school administrators, special education professionals, and parents/guardians work together to design and execute the IEP.

> **THE FAMILY EDUCATIONAL RIGHTS AND PRIVACY ACT (1974):** also known as the Buckley Amendment, this law assures confidentiality of student records

Due Process

THE FAMILY EDUCATIONAL RIGHTS AND PRIVACY ACT (1974), also known as the Buckley Amendment, assures confidentiality of student records. Parents are afforded the right to examine, review, request changes in information deemed inaccurate, and stipulate persons who might access their child's records. "Due process is a set of procedures designed to ensure the fairness of educational decisions and the accountability of both professionals and parents in making these decisions" (Kirk and Gallagher, 1986, p. 24). These procedures serve as a mechanism by which the student and his or her family can voice their opinions, concerns, or dissents. Due process safeguards exist in all matters pertaining to identification, evaluation, and educational placement.

Types of due process

Due process occurs in two realms, substantive and procedural. Substantive due process is the content of the law (e.g. appropriate placement for special education students). Procedural due process is the form through which substantive due process is carried out (i.e., parental permission for testing). Public Law 101-476 contains many items of both substantive and procedural due process.

1. A due process hearing may be initiated by parents or the local educational agency (LEA) as an impartial forum for challenging decisions about identification, evaluation, or placement. Either party may present evidence, cross-examine witnesses, obtain a record of the hearing, and be advised by counsel or by individuals having expertise in the education of individuals with disabilities. Findings may be appealed to the state education agency (SEA) and if still dissatisfied, either party may bring civil action in a state of federal district court. Hearing timelines are set by legislation.

2. Parents may obtain an independent evaluation if there is disagreement about the education evaluation performed by the LEA. The results of such an evaluation must be considered in any decision made with respect to the provision of a free, appropriate public education for the student, and may be presented as evidence at a hearing. Further, the parents may request this evaluation at public expense if a hearing officer requests an independent educational evaluation, or if the decision from a due process hearing is that the LEA's evaluation was inappropriate. If the final decision holds that, the evaluation performed is appropriate, the parent has still the right to an independent educational evaluation, but not as public expense.

3. Written notice must be provided to parents prior to a proposal or refusal to initiate or make a change in the student's identification, evaluation, or educational placement.

   - A listing of parental due process safeguards.

   - A description and a rationale for the chosen action.

   - A detailed listing of components (e.g., tests, records, reports) which was the basis for the decision.

   - Assurance that the language and content of notices were understood by the parents.

4. Parental consent must be obtained before evaluation procedures can occur, unless there is a state law specifying otherwise.

5. Sometimes parents or guardians cannot be identified to function in the due process role. When this occurs, a suitable person must be assigned to act as a surrogate. This is done by the LEA in full accordance with legislation.

Inclusion, Mainstreaming, and Least Restrictive Environment

Inclusion, mainstreaming, and least restrictive environment are interrelated policies under IDEA, with varying degrees of statutory imperatives, which include:

* Inclusion is the right of students with disabilities to be placed in regular classrooms

* Least restrictive environment is the mandate that students be educated with their nondisabled peers to the maximum extent appropriate

* Mainstreaming is a policy where disabled students can be placed in the regular classroom, as long as such placement does not interfere with the student's educational plan

Sample Test Questions and Rationale

(Easy)

1. Which of the following does the least to address the needs of students with disabilities?

   A. IDEA

   B. Title IX

   C. P.L. 94-142

   D. Least restrictive environment

The answer is B.

The U.S. Constitution does not specify protection for education. However, all states provide education, and thus individuals are guaranteed protection and due process under the 14th Amendment. The basic source of law for special education is the Individuals with Disabilities Education Act (IDEA) and its accompanying regulations. After segregation was outlawed by the decision from *Brown v. Board of Education*, parents and other advocates filed similar lawsuits on behalf of students with special needs. The culmination of their efforts resulted in P.L. 94-142. The definition of a least restrictive environment (LRE) differs with each student's needs. LRE means that the student is placed in an environment that is not dangerous or overly controlling or intrusive.

(Average)

2. Free appropriate education, the individual education program, procedural safeguards, and least restrictive environment; identify the legislation represented by these elements.

   A. Americans with Disabilities Act

   B. The Equal Access Act

   C. The Individuals with Disabilities Education Act

   D. Title VI, The Civil Rights Act of 1964

The answer is C.

The Individuals with Disabilities Education Act (IDEA) requires that all states receiving federal funding provide mandatory education programs for students with disabilities. P.L. 94-142 was reenacted as IDEA and the elements listed represent its key concepts.

SKILL 2.4 Knows approaches for accommodating various learning styles, intelligences, or exceptionalities

A teacher must acknowledge the variety of learning styles and abilities among students within a class (and, indeed, the varieties from class to class) and apply multiple instructional and assessment processes to ensure that every child has appropriate opportunities to master the subject matter, demonstrate such mastery, and improve and enhance learning skills with each lesson.

No two students are alike. It follows, then, that no students learn alike. To apply a one-dimensional instructional approach and have strict tunnel vision is to impose learning limits on students. All students have the right to an education, but there cannot be a singular path to that education. A teacher must acknowledge the variety of learning styles and abilities among students within a class (and, indeed, the varieties from class to class) and apply multiple instructional and assessment processes to ensure that every student has appropriate opportunities to master the subject matter, demonstrate such mastery, and improve and enhance learning skills with each lesson.

Differentiated Instruction

DIFFERENTIATED INSTRUCTION (DI): the concept that since students have different ways of learning, teachers must utilize different methods of teaching

It is difficult to define intelligence, but teachers know and recognize the differences in the intelligence of their students. This complicates the development of DIFFERENTIATED INSTRUCTION (DI). Some of the student from homes where reading, books, and learning are not a high priority will, nevertheless, rank high on the intelligence scale as will some where parents seem indifferent to their children's progress. Some will be very low on this scale regardless of background. It is very challenging to develop teaching approaches and methods that will make certain none of the students are left behind. Should a teacher choose the lowest common denominator and ignore the likelihood that many of the students in the class could grasp highly abstract ideas and concepts, or is it better to aim for the middle and hope for the best?

Accepting students' differences

A committed educator not only accepts students' differences but also acts on them by differentiating his or her instructional practices. This means that differentiating instruction is not something done on Fridays; it is what effective teachers do every day in the classroom so that every student's learning needs are met. According to well-respected DI proponent Carol Ann Tomlinson, differentiation "occurs as teachers become increasingly proficient in understanding their students as individuals, increasingly comfortable with the meaning and structure of the disciplines they teach, and increasingly expert at teaching flexibly in order to match instruction to student need with the goal of maximizing the potential of each learner in a given area."

Understanding students

Teachers who differentiate their instruction begin by developing a broad and thorough understanding of their students. Gathering this data about students and using it to purposefully implement differentiated practices can be time consuming and cumbersome, especially as greater demands and expectations squeeze into teachers' already tight schedules. However, by promoting the focused and deliberate integration of technology, these challenging and sometimes difficult tasks can become both practical and increasingly more manageable in the differentiated classroom.

Implementing DI in the classroom

The effective teacher will seek to connect all students to the subject matter through multiple techniques, with the goal that each student, through their own abilities, will relate to one or more techniques and excel in the learning process. Differentiated instruction encompasses several areas:

- Content: What is the teacher going to teach? Or, perhaps better put, what does the teacher want the students to learn? Differentiating content means that students will have access to content that piques their interest about a topic, with a complexity that provides an appropriate challenge for their intellectual development.

- Process: This is a classroom management technique where instructional organization and delivery is maximized for the diverse student group. These techniques should include dynamic, flexible grouping activities, where instruction and learning occurs as whole-class units, teacher-led activities, and peer learning and teaching (while teacher observes and coaches) within small groups or pairs.

- Product: There are expectations and requirements placed on students to demonstrate their knowledge or understanding. The type of product expected from each student should reflect each student's own capabilities.

The effective teacher will seek to connect all students to the subject matter through multiple techniques, with the goal that each student, through their own abilities, will relate to one or more techniques and excel in the learning process.

Cooperative Learning

Cooperative learning situations, as practiced in today's classrooms, grew out of research studies in the early 1970s. Cooperative learning situations can range from very formal applications such as Student Teams-Achievement Divisions (STAD) and Cooperative Integrated Reading and Composition (CIRC) to less formal groupings known variously as group investigation, learning together, or discovery groups. Cooperative learning as a general term is now firmly recognized and established as a teaching and learning technique in American schools.

Implementing cooperative learning in the classroom

COOPERATIVE LEARNING: an approach to learning that focuses on students working together to solve problems

COOPERATIVE LEARNING techniques are widely diffused in schools; therefore, it is necessary to orient students in the skills by which cooperative learning groups can operate smoothly, and thereby enhance learning. Students who cannot interact constructively with other students will not be able to take advantage of the learning opportunities provided by the cooperative learning situations and will furthermore deprive their fellow students of the opportunity for cooperative learning. These skills form the hierarchy of cooperation in which students first learn to work together as a group, they may then proceed to levels at which they may engage in simulated-conflict situations. This cooperative setting allows different points of view to be entertained constructively.

Alternative Assessments

ALTERNATIVE ASSESSMENTS: allow students to create an answer or a response to a question or task

ALTERNATIVE ASSESSMENTS allow students to create an answer or a response to a question or task. This is as opposed to traditional, inflexible assessments where students choose a response from among a prepared selection, such as matching, multiple-choice, or true/false. Efforts to develop useful alternatives to standardized testing have proliferated during the past several years. Few current movements have caught the attention of educators as quickly as the move toward more direct assessment of student performance.

Several labels have been used to describe alternatives to standardized tests. The most common include direct assessment, authentic assessment, performance assessment, and the more generic alternative assessment. Proponents feel that sampling tiny snippets of student behavior does not provide insight into how students would perform on truly worthy intellectual tasks and that student learning can be better assessed by examining and judging a student's actual (or simulated) performance on significant, relevant tasks.

Implementing alternative assessments in the classroom

When implemented effectively, an alternative assessment approach will exhibit these characteristics, among others:

- Requires higher-order thinking and problem-solving

- Provides opportunities for student self-reflection and self-assessment

- Uses real-world applications to connect students to the subject

- Provides opportunities for students to learn and examine subjects on their own, as well as to collaborate with their peers.

- Encourages students to continuing learning beyond the requirements of the assignment

- Clearly defines objective and performance goals

Testing Modifications

The intent of testing modifications is to minimize the effect of a student's disability or learning challenge. This provides an equal opportunity for students with disabilities to participate in assessments to demonstrate and express their knowledge and ability.

Testing modifications should be identified in the student's IEP, consistently implemented, and used to the least extent possible. Types of testing modifications include:

- Flexible scheduling: providing time extensions or altering testing duration (e.g., by inserting appropriate breaks)

- Flexible setting: using special lighting or acoustics, minimizing distractions (e.g., testing the student in a separate location), using adaptive equipment

- Alternate test format: using large print or Braille, increasing the space allocated for student response, realigning the format of question and answer selections (e.g., vertically rather than horizontally)

- Use of mechanical aids: tape recorders, word processors, visual and auditory magnification devices, calculators, spell check and grammar check software (where spelling and grammar are not the focus of the assessment)

Sample Test Question and Rationale

(Rigorous)

1. When students provide evidence of having special needs, standardized tests can be:

   A. Given out with the same predetermined questions as what is administered to students without special needs

   B. Exempted for certain students whose special-needs conditions would prevent them performing with any reliability or validity

   C. Administered over a lengthier test period (i.e., four hours instead of three or two)

   D. All of the above

The answer is D.

The intent of testing modifications is to minimize the effect of a student's disability or learning challenge. This provides an equal opportunity for students with disabilities to participate in assessments to demonstrate and express their knowledge and ability. However, if the student's special-needs conditions would prevent them performing with any reliability or validity, they should be exempted from taking the assessment.

SKILL 2.5 Knows the process of second-language acquisition and strategies to support the learning of students for whom English is not a first language

One of the most important things to know about the differences between first language (L1) and second language (L2) acquisition is that people usually will master L1, but they will almost never be fully proficient in L2.

One of the most important things to know about the differences between first language (L1) and second language (L2) acquisition is that people usually will master L1, but they will almost never be fully proficient in L2. However, if children can be trained in L2 before the age of seven, their chances at full mastery will be much higher. Children learn languages with little effort, which is why they can be babbling during one year and speaking with complete, complex ideas just a few years later. It is important to know that language is innate, meaning that our brains are ready to learn a language from birth. Yet a lot of language learning is behavioral, meaning that children imitate adults' speech.

L2 Acquisition

L2 acquisition is much harder for adults. Multiple theories of L2 acquisition have been developed by researchers such as Jim Cummins. Cummins argues that there are two types of language that usually need to be acquired by students learning English as a second language: Basic Interpersonal Communication Skills (BICS) and Cognitive Academic Language Proficiency (CALP). BICS is general, everyday language used to communicate simple thoughts. In contrast, CALP is the more complex, academic language used in school. It is harder for students to acquire CALP, and many teachers mistakenly assume that students can learn complex academic concepts in English if they have already mastered BICS. The truth is that CALP takes much longer to master, and in some cases, particularly with little exposure in certain subjects, it may never be mastered.

Five principles of L2 aquisition

Another set of theories is based on Stephen Krashen's research in L2 acquisition. Most people understand his theories based on five principles:

ACQUISITION-LEARNING HYPOTHESIS: suggests that there is a difference between learning a language and acquiring it

MONITOR HYPOTHESIS: suggests that the learned language "monitors" the acquired language; a person's "grammar check" kicks in and keeps awkward, incorrect language out of a person's L2 communication

1. The **ACQUISITION-LEARNING HYPOTHESIS:** This states that there is a difference between learning a language and acquiring it. Children "acquire" a first language easily—it's natural. But adults often have to "learn" a language through coursework, studying, and memorizing. One can acquire a second language, but often it requires more deliberate and natural interaction with that language.

2. The **MONITOR HYPOTHESIS:** This is when the learned language "monitors" the acquired language. In other words, this is when a person's "grammar check" kicks in and keeps awkward, incorrect language out of a person's L2 communication.

3. The NATURAL ORDER HYPOTHESIS: This suggests that the learning of grammatical structures is predictable and follows a "natural order."

4. The INPUT HYPOTHESIS: Some people call this "comprehensible input." This means that a language learner will learn best when the instruction or conversation is just above the learner's ability. That way, the learner has the foundation to understand most of the language, but will still have to figure out, often in context, what the more difficult elements mean.

5. The AFFECTIVE FILTER HYPOTHESIS: This suggests that people will learn a second language when they are relaxed, have high levels of motivation, and have a decent level of self-confidence.

English as a Second Language

Teaching students who are learning English as a second language poses some unique challenges, particularly in a standards-based environment. The key is realizing that no matter how little English a student knows, the teacher should teach with the student's developmental level in mind. This means that instruction should not be "dumbed-down" for ESOL students. Different approaches should be used, however, to ensure that these students get multiple opportunities to learn and practice English and still learn content.

Approaches to ESOL students

Many ESOL approaches are based on social learning methods. By being placed in mixed level groups or by being paired with a student of another ability level, students will get a chance to practice English in a natural, non-threatening environment. Students should not be pushed into these groups to use complex language or to experiment with words that are too difficult. They should simply get a chance to practice with simple words and phrases.

Additional accommodations for ESOL students

ESOL students may need additional accommodations with assessments, assignments, and projects. For example, teachers may find that written tests provide little to no information about a student's understanding of the content. Therefore, an oral test may be better suited for ESOL students. When students are somewhat comfortable and capable with written tests, a shortened test may actually be preferable; take note that they will need extra time to translate.

Most lay people believe that in high school and college, learning a language involves strictly drills, memorization, and tests. While this is a common method used (some people call it a structural, grammatical, or linguistic approach), it certainly does not work for all students.

NATURAL ORDER HYPOTHESIS: suggests that the learning of grammatical structures is predictable and follows a "natural order"

INPUT HYPOTHESIS: suggests that a language learner will learn best when the instruction or conversation is just above the learner's ability

AFFECTIVE FILTER HYPOTHESIS: suggests that people will learn a second language when they are relaxed, have high levels of motivation, and have a decent level of self-confidence

In teacher-directed instructional situations, visual aids, such as pictures, objects, and video, are particularly effective in helping students make connections between words and items with which they are already familiar.

Motivational approaches to ESOL students

There are many approaches that are noted for their motivational purposes. In a general sense, when teachers work to motivate students to learn a language, they do things to help reduce fear and to assist students in identifying with native speakers of the target language. A very common method is often called the functional approach. In this approach, the teacher focuses on communicative elements. For example, a first-grade ESOL teacher might help students learn phrases that will assist them in finding a restroom, asking for help on the playground, etc. Many functionally based adult ESOL programs help learners with travel-related phrases and words.

Total physical response

> **TOTAL PHYSICAL RESPONSE:** a kinesthetic approach that combines language learning and physical movement

Another very common motivational approach is TOTAL PHYSICAL RESPONSE. This is a kinesthetic approach that combines language learning and physical movement. In essence, students learn new vocabulary and grammar by responding to verbal commands with physical motion. Some people say it is particularly effective because the physical actions create good brain connections with the words.

In general, the best methods do not treat students as if they have a language deficit. Rather, the best methods build upon what students already know, and they help to instill the target language as a communicative process rather than a list of vocabulary words that have to be memorized.

Sample Test Question and Rationale

(Easy)

1. **What is one of the most important things to know about the differences between first language (L1) and second language (L2) acquisition?**

   A. A second language is easier to acquire than a first language

   B. Most people master a second language (L2) , but rarely do they master a first language (L1)

   C. Most people master a first language (L1), but rarely do they master a second language (L2)

   D. Acquiring a first language (L1) takes the same level of difficulty as acquiring a second language (L2)

The answer is C.

One of the most important things to know about the differences between first language (L1) and second language (L2) acquisition is that people usually will master L1, but they will almost never be fully proficient in L2.

SKILL 2.6 Understands the influence of individual experiences, talents, and prior learning, as well as language, culture, family, and community values on student learning

What city doesn't have restaurants that represent countries around the world— Italian, Chinese, Japanese, Mexican, Jamaican, etc.? The same is true of America's classrooms. Even in small towns, school classrooms tend to showcase the melting pot that makes up twenty-first century American culture. The challenge of our schools is to educate all students with equality, fairness, and success.

Diversity can be further defined as:

- Differences among learners, classroom settings, and academic outcomes

- Biological, sociological, ethnicity, socioeconomic status, psychological needs, and learning preferences and styles among learners

- Differences in classroom settings that promote learning opportunities such as collaborative, participatory, and individualized learning groups

- Expected learning outcomes that are theoretical, affective, and cognitive for students

Addressing Diversity in the Classroom

Effective teaching and learning for students begins with teachers who can demonstrate an appreciation for diversity in relationships and within school communities.

Effective teaching and learning for students begins with teachers who can demonstrate an appreciation for diversity in relationships and within school communities. It is an old-fashioned notion, but true nonetheless: teachers are models, whether or not they choose to be. Students will imitate the teacher who leads with honesty. If the teacher is only pretending to like students, the student will know it. If that teacher is sensitive and caring, many of the challenges presented by a diverse classroom will be well managed.

At the same time, teachers must be in charge. They must be firm classroom leaders who are serious about their roles in preparing their young charges for the challenges they will face as they grow. Effective teachers use instructional techniques that enable students to enjoy learning and feel comfortable in the educational environment.

COMPETENCY 3
STUDENT MOTIVATION AND THE LEARNING ENVIRONMENT

SKILL 3.1 Knows theoretical foundations of human motivation and behavior

MOTIVATION: an internal state that activates, guides, and sustains behavior

MOTIVATION is an internal state that activates, guides, and sustains behavior. Research in educational psychology describes motivation as the volition or will that students bring to a task, their level of interest and intrinsic persistence, the personally held goals that guide their behavior, and their belief about the causes of their success or failure.

Motivational Theories

A form of attribution theory developed by Bernard Weiner (2000) describes how students' beliefs about the causes of academic success or failure affect their emotions and motivations; "Interpersonal and intrapersonal theories of motivation from an attributional perspective" (*Educational Psychology Review, 12*, pp. 1–14). For example, when students attribute failure to lack of ability, and ability is perceived as uncontrollable, they experience the emotions of shame and embarrassment and consequently decrease effort and show poorer performance. In contrast, when students attribute failure to lack of effort, and effort is perceived as controllable, they experience the emotion of guilt and consequently increase effort and show improved performance.

Learners' goals in motivational theories

Motivational theories also explain how learners' goals affect the way they engage in academic tasks. Those who have MASTERY GOALS strive to increase their ability and knowledge. Those who have PERFORMANCE APPROACH GOALS strive for high grades and seek opportunities to demonstrate their abilities. Those who have PERFORMANCE AVOIDANCE GOALS are driven by fear of failure and avoid situations where their abilities are exposed. Research has found that mastery goals are associated with many positive outcomes such as persistence in the face of failure, preference for challenging tasks, creativity, and intrinsic motivation. Performance avoidance goals are associated with negative outcomes such as poor concentration while studying, disorganized studying, less self-regulation, shallow information processing, and test anxiety. Performance approach goals are associated with positive outcomes and some negative outcomes such as an unwillingness to seek help and shallow information processing.

MASTERY GOALS: characterized by students who strive to increase their ability and knowledge

PERFORMANCE APPROACH GOALS: characterized by students who strive for high grades and seek opportunities to demonstrate their abilities

PERFORMANCE AVOIDANCE GOALS: characterized by students who are driven by fear of failure and avoid situations where their abilities are exposed

---

SKILL 3.2 Knows how knowledge of human motivation and behavior should influence strategies for organizing and supporting individual and group work in the classroom

---

Applied behavior analysis is effective in a range of educational settings and is a set of techniques based on the behavioral principles of operant conditioning. For example, teachers can improve student behavior by systematically rewarding students who follow classroom rules with praise, stars, or tokens. These strategies are known as EXTRINSIC MOTIVATORS. Despite the demonstrated efficacy of awards in changing behavior, their use in education has been criticized by proponents of self-determination theory, who claim that praise and other rewards undermine intrinsic motivation. In addition, some educators argue that

EXTRINSIC MOTIVATORS: strategies that are characterized by motivating students through utilizing rewards for good behavior

extrinsic motivation is not typically an effective strategy to build intrinsic motivation.

Affecting intrinsic motivation

In fact, there is evidence that tangible rewards decrease intrinsic motivation in specific situations, such as when the student already has a high level of intrinsic motivation to perform the goal behavior. Results showing detrimental effects are counterbalanced by evidence that, in other situations, such as when rewards are given for attaining a gradually increasing standard of performance, rewards enhance intrinsic motivation.

Sample Test Question and Rationale

(Rigorous)

1. **Mrs. Grant is providing her students with many extrinsic motivators in order to increase their intrinsic motivation. Which of the following best explains this relationship?**

   A. This is a good relationship and will increase intrinsic motivation

   B. The relationship builds animosity between the teacher and the students

   C. Extrinsic motivation does not in itself help to build intrinsic motivation

   D. There is no place for extrinsic motivation in the classroom

The answer is C.

There are some cases where it is necessary to utilize extrinsic motivation; however, the use of extrinsic motivation is not typically an effective strategy to build intrinsic motivation. Intrinsic motivation comes from within students themselves, while extrinsic motivation comes from external individuals/forces.

> **SKILL 3.3** Knows factors and situations that are likely to promote or diminish student's motivation to learn, and how to help students to become self-motivated

Teachers need to be aware that much of what they say and do can be motivating and may have a positive effect on students' achievement. Studies have been conducted to determine the impact of teacher behavior on student performance. Surprisingly, a teacher's voice can make a real impression on students. The human voice has several dimensions, including volume, pitch, rate, etc. A recent study on the effects of speech rate indicates that, although both boys and girls prefer to listen at a rate of about 200 words per minute, boys tend to prefer slower rates than girls. This same study indicates that a slower rate of speech directly affects processing ability and comprehension.

> *Teachers need to be aware that much of what they say and do can be motivating and may have a positive effect on students' achievement.*

Teachers as Motivators

Other speech factors correlate with teaching-criterion scores including:

- Communication of ideas

- Communication of emotion

- Distinctness/pronunciation

- Quality variation and phrasing

These scores show that "good" teachers ("good" meaning teachers who positively impact and motivate students) use more variety in speech than do less effective teachers. Thus, a teacher's speech skills can be strong motivating elements. Body language has an even greater effect on student achievement and ability to set and focus on goals. Smiles provide support and give feedback about the teacher's affective state—a deadpan expression can actually be detrimental to student progress, and frowns are perceived by students to mean displeasure, disapproval, and even anger. Studies also show that teacher posture and movement are indicators of their enthusiasm and energy, which emphatically influence student outcomes including learning, attitudes, motivation, and focus on goals. Teachers are second only to parents in their effect on student motivation.

Hands-on learning

Teachers can also enhance student motivation by planning and directing interactive, hands-on learning experiences. Research substantiates that cooperative group projects decrease student behavior problems and increase student on-task behavior. Students who are directly involved with learning activities are more motivated to complete a task to the best of their ability.

Sample Test Question and Rationale

(Easy)

1. **A teacher's posture and movement affect the following student outcomes except:**

    A. Student learning

    B. Attitudes

    C. Motivation

    D. Physical development

The answer is D.

Studies show that a teacher's posture and movement are indicators of their enthusiasm and energy, which emphatically influence student outcomes including learning, attitudes, motivation, and focus on goals.

SKILL 3.4 Knows principles of effective classroom management and strategies to promote positive relationships, cooperation, and purposeful learning

When a teacher receives a new group of students, rules should be established immediately. Students should be involved as much as possible in the formulation and discussion of the rules and why they are necessary. By helping to establish the policies, they will be more likely to assume responsibility for following them. Once the rules are established, enforcement and reinforcement should begin right away.

Implementation of Classroom Rules

Approximately four to six classroom rules should be posted where students can easily see and read them. They should be stated positively, describe specific behaviors, and be easy to understand. Certain rules may also be tailored for individual students to meet target goals or IEP requirements. For example, a new student who has had problems with leaving the classroom may need an individual behavioral contract to assist him/her with adjusting to the class rule about remaining in the assigned area.

Introduction of rules

The teacher should clarify and model the expected behavior. In addition to the general classroom management plan, a management plan should be developed for special situations, (i.e., fire drills) and transitions (i.e., going to and from the cafeteria). Periodic review of the rules, as well as modeling and practice, may be conducted as needed, such as after an extended school holiday.

Consequences and rewards

When the rules are introduced, CONSEQUENCES should be discussed, clearly stated, and understood by all of the students. The severity of the consequence should match the severity of the offense and must be enforceable. The teacher must apply the consequence consistently and fairly; in that way, the students will know what to expect when they choose to break a rule.

Like consequences, students should understand what rewards to expect for following the rules. The teacher should never promise a reward that cannot be delivered and should follow through with the reward as soon as possible. Consistency and fairness are also necessary for rewards to be effective. Students will become frustrated and give up if they see that rewards and consequences are not delivered in a timely and fair manner.

Adapt for Transitions

Transitions refer to changes in class activities that involve movement. Some examples of transitions are:

1. Breaking up from large group instruction and moving into small groups for learning centers and small-group instructions

2. Moving from classroom to lunch, to the playground, or to elective classes

3. Finishing reading at the end of one period and getting ready for math the next period

4. Emergency situations such as fire drills

Successful transitions are achieved by using PROACTIVE STRATEGIES. Early in the year, the teacher pinpoints the transition periods in the day and anticipates possible behavioral problems, such as students habitually returning late from lunch. After identifying possible problems with the environment or the schedule, the teacher plans proactive strategies to minimize or eliminate those problems. Proactive planning also gives the teacher the advantage of being prepared, addressing behaviors before they become problems, and incorporating strategies into the classroom management plan right away. When transition plans are developed for each type of transition, the students can be taught the expected behaviors for each situation.

> **PROACTIVE STRATEGIES:** preventative strategies that address behaviors before they become problems

PLAN FOR SUCCESSFUL TRANSITIONS	
Identify the Specific Behaviors Needed for the Type of Transition	For example, during a fire drill, students must quickly leave the classroom, walk quietly as a group to the designated exit, proceed to the assigned waiting area, stay with the group, wait for the teacher to receive the all-clear signal, walk quickly and quietly back to the classroom with the group, and reenter the classroom and return to their seats.
Develop a Set of Expectations and Teach Them to the Students	Written behavioral expectations should use language that is positive and specific. Establish a rationale for the rules and provide an explanation of the rules. Provide corrective feedback and reinforcement to the students who demonstrate knowledge of the rules.
Model the Appropriate Behavior	Guide the students through the procedures and give reinforcement to those who correctly model the behavior.
Have the Students Practice the Behaviors Independently	As students practice behaviors, continue corrective feedback and reinforcement. Certain situations, like fire drills, will not be practiced daily; however, students will have daily opportunities to demonstrate appropriate transitional behavior in and out of class.

Behavior Management

Many factors contribute to student on-task behavior including student interest in the content, student ability, student attitude, and student needs. Teacher behavior can impact student behavior just as strongly as any other factor. It is imperative that teachers use strategies that encourage and maintain on-task behavior and be aware that they alone may be working to motivate students.

It is imperative that teachers use strategies that encourage and maintain on-task behavior and be aware that they alone may be working to motivate students.

Reinforcing and maintaining on-task behavior

A natural way to reinforce on-task behavior is for the teacher to plan activities that reflect student's interests and build lessons based on student's ideas. Teachers guide students through lessons by:

- Responding to their questions and ideas

- Engaging them in conversation

- Challenging their thinking

Once a student-centered foundation has been established for presenting a lesson, the teacher must concentrate on maintaining student focus. To some degree teachers can rely on students' internal motivation to acquire competence. This internal motivation can be greatly affected by the teacher's attitude and enthusiasm; the teacher is a vital role model for promoting student motivation.

The role of questioning

Questioning can help maintain focus, direct academic discussions, and create interactive instruction. Questioning can also reinforce content and sustain both on-task behavior and student motivation. Asking questions is a significant part of the instructional process and is most effective when it includes both simple comprehension questions and complex higher-order-thinking questions.

Feedback for Students

Teacher academic feedback exists in many forms. For instance, verbal response can be an effective positive reinforcement and may contribute to students' on-task behavior. If academic feedback is specific, evaluative, and/or provides corrective information, then on-task behavior, student motivation, and achievement will increase. The most frequently used types of academic feedback are:

- Giving simple praise

- Repeating what the student has said in an approving manner

- Calling on a student to further develop a response

Academic praise or specific statements that give information about the value of a student's response further add to student motivation and on-task behavior

Giving effective feedback

Academic feedback is also effective when it is written, consists of specific comments on errors, and tempered by suggestions as to how the student may improve. It is most productive when it includes at least one positive remark on work done well. It is sometimes difficult to provide written feedback immediately and this delay reduces the effectiveness of the feedback. This is one area where a computer can be more dynamic than a teacher because the computer can provide immediate written feedback.

The Organized Classroom

Instructional momentum requires an organized system to place and distribute supplies and materials. Inability to find an overhead transparency, a necessary chart page, or the handout worksheet for the day not only stops the momentum, but is very irritating to students. When classroom materials cannot be found, this is frustrating for both teacher and students. Many performance-measurement instruments have major categories such as "Handles materials well" and "Maintains instructional momentum."

Grade level differences

In the lower grades, an organized system can include a classroom helper. This student can effectively distribute and collect books, equipment, supplies, etc. The classroom helpers should be taught to replace the materials in the proper places to obtain them easily for future use. Periodically, the teacher should inspect to see that all materials are in the proper places and are ready for use.

At higher grade levels, the teacher is concerned with materials such as textbooks, written instructional aids, worksheets, computer programs, etc. These must be produced, maintained, distributed, and collected for future use. Teachers must have sufficient copies of duplicated materials to satisfy classroom needs. Materials can either be distributed as students are in their learning sites (desks, etc.) or at a clearly specified place (or small number of places) in the classroom. In any case, there should be firmly established procedures, completely understood by students for obtaining classroom materials.

Use time efficiently

For the classroom, punctuality is defined as a "teacher beginning class work promptly." Effective teachers also use classtime efficiently. This results in higher student subject engagement and subject matter retention. One way that teachers use class time efficiently is through management transition, moving smoothly in a systemic, academically oriented way, from one activity to another. Another factor is sometimes defined as "management of instructional material, a teacher's ability to prepare materials…for a particular segment of instruction… (and have them) readily available." In other words, if a teacher is going to use a map in a lesson, copies are prepared and in place before class begins. This results in the efficient distribution of materials and leads to less off-task time.

Establish routines

Effective teachers deal with daily classroom procedures efficiently and quickly, then students will spend the majority of class time engaged in academic tasks, which will likely result in higher achievement. For instance, in taking attendance, a seating chart is effective; absentees can be spotted in seconds by noting the empty seats, rather than calling each student's name. By laminating the seating chart, the teacher can make daily notes right on the chart. He or she may also efficiently keep track of who is volunteering and who is answering questions. This information can create an equitable classroom climate for all students.

Other housekeeping tasks create an efficient classroom when a teacher routinizes activities such as passing papers out, moving to get books, writing on the board, etc., and has materials prepared, procedures worked out, and everything in order. Further, teachers should presort papers into rows and have the first person in the row distribute them. Instructing the students of the daily routine activities early in the year leads to a more efficient use of class time on a daily basis.

Sample Test Questions and Rationale

(Average)

1. **Which statement is an example of specific individual praise?**

   A. "John, you are the only person in class not paying attention."

   B. "William, I thought we agreed that you would turn in all of your homework."

   C. "Robert, you did a good job staying in line. See how it helped us get to music class on time."

   D. "Class, you did a great job cleaning up the art room."

   The answer is C.

   Praise is a powerful tool in obtaining and maintaining order in a classroom. In addition, it is an effective motivator. It is even more effective if the praise is specific and the positive results of good behavior are included.

(Rigorous)

2. **In the classroom, the concept of management transition describes:**

   A. How the administration switches between the principal and vice principal

   B. How parents are prepared for when their children move from one grade to the next

   C. How students monitor the time they spend moving from class to class

   D. How teachers use time effectively so the class moves smoothly from one activity to another

   The answer is D.

   One way teachers use class time efficiently is through "management transition," moving smoothly in a systemic, academically oriented way, from one activity to another.

Sample Test Questions and Rationale (cont.)

(Easy)

3. A laminated seating chart can assist teachers in simplifying all of the following tasks except:

   A. Performing self-assessments

   B. Taking attendance

   C. Making daily notes

   D. Keeping track of participation

The answer is A.

Seating charts can assist teachers in taking attendance; absentees can be spotted in seconds by noting the empty seats, rather than calling each student's name. By laminating the seating chart, the teacher can make daily notes right on the chart. He or she may also efficiently keep track of who is volunteering and who is answering questions. This information can create an equitable classroom climate for all students.

DOMAIN II
INSTRUCTION AND ASSESSMENT

PERSONALIZED STUDY PLAN

COMPETENCY 4
INSTRUCTIONAL STRATEGIES

Teachers should have a toolkit of instructional strategies, materials, and technologies to teach and encourage students to problem solve and think critically about subject content. When districts choose a curriculum, it is expected that students will master established benchmarks and standards of learning. Research of national and state standards indicates that there are additional benchmarks and learning objectives measured in all state assessments. These apply to most subjects including science, foreign language, English/language arts, history, art, health, civics, economics, geography, physical education, mathematics, and social studies (Marzano & Kendall, 1996).

Critical Thinking

It is important that students develop critical thinking skills. When a student learns to think critically, he or she learns how to apply knowledge to a specific subject area; but more importantly, the student knows how to apply that information in other subject areas. For example, in algebra, students must be taught the order of numerical expressions. To foster critical thinking, the teacher would teach the concept and then provide a math word problem for students to compute the amount of material needed to build a fence around an eight-by-twelve-foot backyard. To solve the problem, students must think critically and group the fencing measurements into an algebraic word problem and perform minor addition, subtraction, and multiplication to determine the amount of material needed. Their new skill could be applied to geography, science, woodworking, sewing, baking, and many tasks that are outside of the mathematics classroom.

Classroom examples of critical thinking

As another example, students use basic reading skills to read passages, math word problems, or project directions. To fully comprehend the material read, however, students must apply additional thinking skills. These higher-order, critical thinking skills operate as students "think about thinking." Teachers are instrumental in helping students use these skills in everyday activities such as:

- Analyzing bills for overcharges

- Comparing shopping ads or catalogue deals

- Finding the main idea from readings

- Applying what's been learned to new situations

- Gathering information/data from a diversity of sources to plan a project

- Following a sequence of directions

- Looking for cause and effect relationships

- Comparing and contrasting information in synthesizing information

Creative and Higher-Ordered Thinking

To create the ultimate environment for creative thinking and continuous learning, teachers should use diversity in instructional strategies, engaging and challenging curricula, and the latest technologies. When teachers are innovative and creative, they model and foster creative thinking in their students. Encouraging students to maintain portfolios from projects and assignments will allow them to make conscious choices to include diverse, creative endeavors that can be treasured throughout their educational journey.

INDIVIDUALIZED PORTFOLIOS: performance-based assessments that allow teachers to chart student's academic and emotional growth

INDIVIDUALIZED PORTFOLIOS are performance-based assessments that allow teachers to chart student's academic and emotional growth. Teachers can also use semester portfolios to gauge progress. This is particularly important for older students who are constantly changing their self-images and worldviews. Through a teacher's guidance, students can master a concept and create a bridge connecting knowledge to application. When this happens, the teacher can share an enjoyable moment of higher-level learning with the student.

By helping students understand the art of visualization and the creativity of discovery, teachers can sow the seeds toward the cure for AIDS, cancer, or reading difficulties.

Ways to encourage higher-ordered thinking

Art can be incorporated into most subjects including reading, math, and science. Mental mind mapping, graphic organizers, and concept web guides are all instructional strategies that teachers can use to guide students into deeper subject matter inquiry. Imagine fostering creativity in students that mimics that of German chemist Fredrich August Kekule; he looked into a fire one night and solved the molecular structure of benzene! By helping students understand the art of visualization and the creativity of discovery, teachers can sow the seeds toward the cure for AIDS, cancer, or reading difficulties.

Other important, life-long educational processes include developing effective note-taking skills, welcoming diverse perspectives, and appreciating the greatest computer on record, the human mind. In addition, teachers should train students to use math manipulatives, a technique for visual processing. Next, the process of journaling can help students understand their own learning. Lastly, when students present information to the class using posters and PowerPoint presentations; these can be powerful, creative methods of teaching and learning.

Inductive and Deductive Thinking

In DEDUCTIVE REASONING or learning, a teacher presents general concepts or principles and provides specific examples supporting the generalizations. INDUCTIVE REASONING occurs in the reverse: a teacher presents information or data and encourages students to hypothesize, identify patterns, draw conclusions, and then finally produce generalizations. This tends to involve students more deeply in the learning process. A teacher should choose the method based on the goals of instruction and the needs of the students.

Examples of inductive and deductive thinking

For example, when mother is working in the kitchen, children conclude that a meal is coming soon; when parents put coats on their kids, they believe that they are going outdoors. These conclusions are drawn not from one observation but from repeated ones. This is inductive thinking: observing particular occurrences and drawing conclusions. Deduction is the opposite. One begins with a conclusion, for example, "all men are mortal," and support the statement with particulars: "Socrates died, Plato died, all the men we have ever known have died; therefore, all men are mortal."

Challenges of inductive and deductive thinking

Sometimes wrong conclusions are drawn on the basis of particulars. There are many legal cases where particular pieces of evidence have been used to find a person guilty in a court of law. However, a significant bit of evidence that comes later, such as the person's DNA, proves that the conclusion of guilt was wrong. Drawing incorrect conclusions are also common when students use inductive and deductive reasoning; therefore, teachers must closely monitor this process for it to be a useful tool in helping students become critical thinkers.

Memorization and Recall

Understanding students' learning styles allows a teacher to share and target specific memorization techniques. These then help students absorb the large quantities of material they are expected to recall and master. For example, MNE-MONICS incorporate rhymes and acronyms and are effective for visual learners. Mnemonics rely not only on repetition to remember facts but also on associations

> **DEDUCTIVE REASONING:** general concepts or principles supported by specific examples

> **INDUCTIVE REASONING:** drawing conclusions from information or data

> *Understanding students' learning styles allows a teacher to share and target specific memorization techniques. These then help students absorb the large quantities of material they are expected to recall and master.*

> **MNEMONICS:** memorization techniques that rely on associations between easy-to-remember constructs and lists of data

between easy-to-remember constructs and lists of data. It is based on the principle that the human mind can more easily recall insignificant data when it is attached (in a logical way) to spatial, personal, or otherwise meaningful information. Kinesthetic learners use their imaginations to create mind-pictures of events and actions. In contrast, auditory learners rely on note taking, review, and recitation to facilitate memorization and recall.

It was once considered a mark of extraordinary intelligence and learning to be able to recite long poems or long selections from books, particularly the Bible. However, simple memorization no longer has the place in education that it once did. Now students are expected to apply their knowledge in new and challenging tasks. Even so, the ability to memorize and recall principles and ideas (even text) is an important attribute of the learned person. Thus, the classroom teacher has an obligation to promote and develop these skills.

Social Reasoning

SOCIAL THEORY refers to the use of theoretical frameworks to explain and analyze social patterns and large-scale social structures. The goal of social reasoning is to see an issue from different perspectives, to understand social and ethical concerns surrounding an issue, and to be able to step back and view the issue as an historian would. A teacher can use questioning on a given issue to strengthen students' social reasoning abilities (e.g., what is the history of this issue and has it changed over time? How do diverse communities view this issue? What are some ethical questions surrounding this issue? Who benefits or is harmed by this issue? What can I [the student] do about this issue?).

> **SOCIAL THEORY:** the use of theoretical frameworks to explain and analyze social patterns and large-scale social structures

Though many researchers consider social theory a branch of sociology, it is inherently interdisciplinary because it uses and contributes to a plethora of disciplines such as anthropology, economics, theology, history, and many others. Social theory attempts to answer the question "What is?" not "What should be?" One should therefore not confuse it with philosophy or with belief.

Representation of Ideas

A visual representation of an idea or concept is a powerful instructional and learning tool. Through these aides, a teacher can provide strong connections and foundations for student understanding. In turn, by producing a visual representation, a student demonstrates his/her understanding of the idea or concept. This ability is often critical in problem analysis and solving, as well as in creative pursuits where hard facts are absent and conceptualization is subjective.

Using visual representations

In society, many people often think of ideas as being represented in words; however, this thinking needs to be expanded. There are so many other means and devices that are available to the teacher. For example, the old adage, "a picture is worth a thousand words" is, in fact, a truism. Students incorporate ideas much better if they have an opportunity to absorb them through more than one sense. For example, when learning a unit on drama or even literature, nothing substitutes for seeing one of Shakespeare's plays performed. Graphs, charts, photographs, paintings, drawings, and videos all represent an idea (or set of ideas).

Sample Test Questions and Rationale

(Easy)

1. **What is the most important benefit of students developing critical thinking skills?**

   A. Students are able to apply knowledge to a specifc subject area as well as other subject areas

   B. Students remember the information for testing purposes

   C. Students focus on a limited number of specific facts

   D. Students do not have to memorize the information for later recall

   The answer is A.

   When a student learns to think critically he or she learns how to apply knowledge to a specific subject area; but more importantly, the student knows how to apply that information in other subject areas.

(Average)

2. **How can mnemonic devices be used to increase achievement?**

   A. They help students learn to pronounce assigned terms

   B. They provide visual cues to help students recall information

   C. They give auditory hints to increase learner retention

   D. They are most effective with kinesthetic learners

   The answer is B.

   Mnemonics rely not only on repetition to remember facts, but also on associations between easy-to-remember constructs and lists of data. It is based on the principle that the human mind can more easily recall insignificant data when it is attached (in a logical way) to spatial, personal, or otherwise meaningful information.

Direct Instruction

DIRECT INSTRUCTION:
teaching method that
emphasizes well-developed
and carefully planned
lessons with small learning
increments

Siegfried Engelmann and Dr. Wesley Becker are among the researchers who proposed **DIRECT INSTRUCTION**, a teaching method that emphasizes well-developed and carefully planned lessons with small learning increments. It assumes that learning outcomes are improved through clear instruction that eliminates misinterpretations. Their approach is currently used by thousands of schools. It recommends that teacher creativity and autonomy be replaced by a willingness to follow certain carefully prescribed instructional practices. At the same time, it encourages hard work, dedication, and commitment to students. It demands that teachers adopt and internalize the belief that all students, if properly taught, can learn.

Discovery Learning

DISCOVERY LEARNING:
learning technique that
involves students solving
problems by using their
own experience and prior
knowledge to determine
what truths can be learned

Beginning at birth, **DISCOVERY LEARNING** is a normal part of growing-up, and this naturally occurring phenomenon can be used to improve classroom outcomes. Discovery learning is based upon inquiry and has been a factor in most human advances. For example, Rousseau constantly questioned his world, particularly the philosophies and theories that were commonly accepted. Dewey, himself a great discoverer, wrote, "There is an intimate and necessary relation between the processes of actual experience and education." Piaget, Bruner, and Papert have all recommended this teaching method.

In discovery learning, students solve problems by using their own experience and prior knowledge to determine what truths can be learned. Bruner wrote "Emphasis on discovery in learning has precisely the effect on the learner of leading him to a constructionist, to organize what he is encountering in a manner not only designed to discover regularity and relatedness, but also to avoid the kind of information drift that fails to keep account of the uses to which information might have to be put."

Whole Group Discussion

Whole group discussion can be used in a variety of settings, but the most common is in the discussion of an assignment. With this strategy, learning is peer-based; thus, students gain a different perspective on the topic, while also learning to respect the ideas of others. One obstacle to this teaching method is that the same students tend to participate or not participate each time. However, with proper teacher guidance during this activity, whole group discussions are highly valuable.

Case Method Learning

Disseminating and integrating knowledge can be achieved effectively by providing opportunities for students to apply what they learn in the classroom to real-life experiences. The CASE METHOD is an instructional strategy that engages students in active discussion about issues and problems of practical application. It can highlight fundamental dilemmas or critical issues and provide a format for role-playing of ambiguous or controversial scenarios. A successful class discussion involves planning on the part of the instructor and preparation on the part of the students. Instructors should communicate this commitment to the students on the first day of class by clearly articulating course expectations. Just as the instructor carefully plans the learning experience, the students must comprehend the assigned reading and show up for class on time, ready to learn.

> **CASE METHOD:** an instructional strategy that engages students in active discussion about issues and problems of practical application

Concept Mapping

Concept mapping is a common tool used by teachers in various disciplines, and many kinds of maps have been developed for this purpose. They are useful devices, but each teacher must determine which is appropriate for use in his/her own classroom. Following is a common map that is used in writing courses:

Concept Mapping

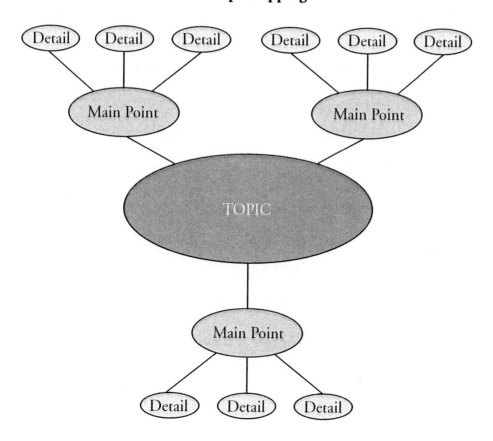

Inquiry

All learning begins with the student. What students know and what they want to learn are not just constraints on what can be taught; they are the very foundation for learning.

DEWEY'S PRIMARY INTERESTS OF THE CHILD
The student's instinctive desire to find things out.
In conversation, the propensity students have to communicate.
In construction, their delight in making things.
Their gifts of artistic expression.

Questioning

Questioning is a teaching strategy as old as Socrates. In fact, the Socratic method is a well-known form of questioning. It is important for the teacher to deliberately and carefully plan in order to lead students in critical thinking.

Play

There are so many educational games available that the most difficult task is choosing which will fit into a classroom. Some are electronic, some are board games, and some are designed to be played by a student individually. Even in those cases, a review of the results by the entire classroom can be a useful learning experience.

Learning Centers

LEARNING CENTERS: an instructional method where students have time during which they can choose their own activity

LEARNING CENTERS are generally used with younger students, but can be extremely important in flexible classrooms. In this set-up, students have some time during which they can choose their own activity. Under a teacher's guidance, learners can even take out-of-class time for creating the centers, collecting the necessary items, and then setting up the area.

Small Group Work

Today's classrooms are usually diverse, and small group work is vital. Students can be grouped according to their developmental level. If the small groups themselves are diverse, this gives students who are struggling an opportunity to learn from students who are already proficient. The better-prepared student will learn from becoming a resource for the weaker student. In turn, the weaker student may sometimes be more likely to accept help from another student. This frees the teacher to perform other tasks.

Revisiting

Revisiting should occur during and at the end of a unit and at the end of a semester. This gives students more than one opportunity to grasp principles and skills and to integrate them.

Reflection

Teaching can move along so rapidly that students may fail to incorporate what they've learned. They may also lack the time to think about what they can bring to the topic. Providing time for reflection and guiding students in developing these tools is a wise teaching method.

Projects

Seeing a unit as a project is also very useful. It opens the door to approaching learning as multitasking. For example, in a unit on birds, not only will students learn about birds, they will have an opportunity to observe them, they can try their hands at drawing them, and they can learn to differentiate one from the other. It's easy to see how a lifetime interest in birdwatching can take root from such a project. This is more effective than simply reading and talking about the topic.

Sample Test Questions and Rationale

(Average)

1. Learning centers are unique instructional tools because they allow students to do all of the following except?

   A. Learn through play

   B. Sit in their seats to complete assignments

   C. Select their own activities

   D. Set up the activity area under a teacher's guidance

   The answer is B.

   Learning centers are extremely important in flexible classrooms. In this set-up, students have some time during which they can choose their own activity. Under a teacher's guidance, learners can even create the centers, collecting the necessary items, and then set up the area.

(Rigorous)

2. Discovery learning is to inquiry as direct instruction is to…

   A. Loosely-developed lessons

   B. Clear instructions

   C. Random lessons

   D. Class discussion

   The answer is B.

   Direct instruction is a teaching method that emphasizes well-developed and carefully planned lessons with small learning increments. It assumes that learning outcomes are improved through clear instruction that eliminates misinterpretations.

(Easy)

3. This instructional strategy engages students in active discussion about issues and problems of practical application.

   A. Case method

   B. Direct instruction

   C. Concept mapping

   D. Formative assessment

   The answer is C.

   The case method is an instructional strategy that engages students in active discussion about issues and problems of practical application.

SKILL 4.3 Knows principles, techniques, and methods associated with major instructional strategies

See Skill 4.2.

SKILL Knows methods for enhancing student learning through the use of
4.4 a variety of resources and materials

*The bridge to effective
student learning begins
when all stakeholders
collaborate.*

Schools cannot underestimate the power and integral role of community institutions. They impact the current and future goals of students, particularly beyond the high school years when they are competing for college access, student internships, and entry-level jobs. Research has shown that students have higher retention, graduation, and higher education–enrollment rates when community institutions are involved and connected with schools. Therefore, to promote tomorrow's citizens, society must reevaluate the current disconnect between the community and its schools.

Community

Community institutions can provide students with meaningful connections and chances for input. This can be accomplished through leadership positions such as the Associated Student Body (ASB), the Parent Teacher Student Association (PTSA), and neighborhood subcommittees addressing political or social issues. In addition, governmental and school boards create avenues for students to explore ethical, participatory, collaborative, and transformational leadership. The lessons learned can then be applied to all areas of students' educational and personal lives.

Student involvement in community

Serving as community liaisons provides students with opportunities to experience accountability and responsibility. In these service positions, students learn about life, how organizations work, effective communications, and teamwork. This teaches students inclusion and social and environmental responsibility. In addition, they learn the importance of creating forums that represent the student voice and vote. Thus, students develop and reflect on individual opinions and begin to understand the dynamics of the world around them.

When support systems are in place, students are able to consistently work on effective teams. They have no fear of taking appropriate risks, such as serving on a local committee about "youth violence" or volunteering in a hospice for young children with terminal diseases. These links to the "real world" provide growth opportunities for students who will soon become integral and vital members. This makes the transition easier for students to become adults.

Local Experts

Most students accept the information shared by teachers; however, not all do. The teacher's credibility expands when students have an opportunity to hear another "expert" talk about the same information. For example, if students are studying water animals, having the director of a fish hatchery talk with the class will increase student interest and understanding. People are usually willing to give their time in this way, and there is reciprocal gain. The person speaking gains satisfaction from passing on his or her own knowledge and expertise, and the students gain a new dimension on the topic being discussed.

Primary Documents

Using primary documents also increases students' interests. In a local history lesson, teachers could use old court house or library documents. This will create interest in the community, its history, and geography, especially if there are old, original maps. While it's not possible to bring the Declaration of Independence into the classroom, facsimiles are available and can have the same result as the original. If students have taken trips to famous places and can report on seeing original documents, this also increases interest.

Field Trip

Parents sometimes see field trips as a ploy for teachers to avoid the responsibility of managing students in the classroom. Nothing could be further from the truth. Some of the richest learning can take place when students have an opportunity to get out of the classroom and participate in an eyes-on, even hands-on, experience related to the topic they are studying.

Service Learning

Service learning has all the advantages of a field trip and also gives students the opportunity to meet another person's needs. For some students, this is when they experience altruism for the first time. Sometimes students are so impacted by this opportunity that they eventually choose service careers. For instance, sometimes students have visited a nursing home and find such fulfillment that they ultimately choose the field of geriatrics for their career.

Technological Resources

The computer system can be divided into two main parts—the hardware and the software. Hardware can be defined as all the physical components that make up the machine. Software includes the programs (sets of instructions) that enable that machine perform particular jobs.

Hardware

INPUT DEVICES are those parts of the computer that accept information from the user. The most common input devices are the keyboard and the mouse. Other more specialized input devices might include joysticks, light pens, touch pads, graphic tablets, voice recognition devices, and optical scanners.

OUTPUT DEVICES are the parts of the computer that display the processing results for the users. These could include the monitor, printers, speakers, plotters, and speech synthesizers. Monitors and printers can vary greatly in the quality of the output displayed. Monitors are classified according to their resolution or dpi (dots per square inch). Super Video Graphics Adapter (SVGA) monitors are able to display a three-dimensional picture that looks almost real.

Printers

Printers vary in the way they produce hard copy as well as in the quality of the final document. The most common found today are ink jet printers, which are generally affordable, and laser printers, which produce superior quality but are also more expensive. They are usually found in offices where quality needs to be high and volume is low.

Storage devices

Storage devices enable computers to save documents and other important files for future use. Internal hard drives provide storage for the large software programs operated on the computer. They are also the most convenient storage for work created. The amount of storage space on a hard drive has become increasingly important as programs increase in size, complexity, and graphic and sound capabilities. By using networks to deliver programs to the individual systems, many schools avoid the limitations imposed by the hard drive's storage space. CD ROM drives and DVD drives access CDs and DVDs that can contain large amounts of information including sound, graphics, and/or video clips.

CPU and RAM

Other components of a computer system are the Central Processing Unit (CPU) and the memory chips on the motherboard. This "brain" of the computer is responsible for receiving input from the input or storage devices, placing it in temporary storage Random Access Memory (RAM), performing any processing functions required by the program (like mathematical equations or sorting), and eventually retrieving the information from storage and displaying it to an output device.

OPERATING SYSTEM PROGRAMS: contain instructions that allow the computer to function

APPLICATION PROGRAMS: facilitate the tasks that a user might wish to perform on the computer

Software

Software consists of all the programs containing instructions for the computer and is stored on a storage device such as the hard drive, CD ROMs, or DVDs. Programs fall into two major groups—operating system or application programs. OPERATING SYSTEM PROGRAMS contain instructions that allow the computer to function. By contrast, APPLICATION PROGRAMS facilitate the tasks that a user might wish to perform on the computer. These might include word processors, databases, spreadsheets, educational and financial programs, games, and telecommunications programs.

Evaluating software

With a surplus of educational software on the market, it is important for an educator to be able to evaluate a program before purchasing it. There are three general steps to follow when evaluating a software program. First, one must read the instructions thoroughly to familiarize oneself with the program, its hardware requirements, and its installation. Once the program is installed and ready to run, the evaluator should use the program from the perspective of a student, without deliberate errors but making use of all the possibilities available to the student. Thirdly, the program should be run making deliberate mistakes to test the handling of errors. The teacher should try to make as many different kinds of mistakes as possible, including making incorrect keyboard entries and ignoring the directions.

Using Computers in Education

A computer lab allieviates the problem of how to give each student access to a computer; however, a whole new set of challenges are introduced. To minimize problems, specific rules should be discussed before the class ever enters the lab. In addition, students should have a thorough understanding of their assignment prior to each session. Expensive hardware can suffer from accidental or deliberate harm if the teacher is not aware of what is going on at all times. Students need to be aware of the consequences for not following the rules because it is so tempting to experiment and show off to their peers.

Computers and research

The computer's ability to store vast amounts of data makes it a great research tool. CD/DVD ROM disks can contain entire encyclopedias, whole classical libraries, or specialized databases on history, science, and the arts. With the "search" feature of these programs, students can type in a one or two word description of the desired topic and the computer will then locate all articles that deal with that subject. Learners can either read the articles on the computer monitor or print them out.

If there is Internet access, the research possibilities are unlimited. When hooked up to the World Wide Web, students can actually talk to people from other parts of the globe or access libraries and journals from all over the world. For example, if students are studying the weather, they might go online and chat with students who live in different climates to compare how weather affects their lives. The students might also access global weather reports, print out weather maps, and discuss their research with meteorologists—all from a single computer station.

Presenting the research

Once the research is completed, a desktop publishing program can be used to produce professional quality documents enhanced by text, graphs, clip art, or photographs. Even primary grade students can use the computer to type and illustrate their stories with simple publishing software like the Children's Writing and Publishing Center by The Learning Company. Spell check and other tools included in these programs can assist students in producing top quality work.

While the computer should not replace teaching traditional research and writing skills, it is a tool that must also be included in the curriculum of students who live in a technological society.

While the computer should not replace teaching traditional research and writing skills, it is a tool that must also be included in the curriculum of students who live in a technological society. Computers are as much a part of a student's life today as pencils and paper. The capabilities of computers need to be thoroughly explored so that students view computers as much more than glorified game machines. A major goal of education is to prepare students for their futures in business and the work place. If they are not taught how to use the available technology to its fullest advantage, educators will have failed in at least part of that purpose.

Networks

A NETWORK is composed of two or more linked computers. More specifically, a computer network is a data communications system made up of hardware and software that transmits data from one computer to another. In part, a computer network includes physical infrastructure like wires, cables, fiber optic lines, undersea cables, and satellites. The other part of a network is the software to keep it running. Computer networks can connect to other computer networks to create a vast computer network.

NETWORK: two or more linked computers

Network configurations

There are numerous configurations for computer networks, including:

- Local-area networks (LANs): the computers are all contained within the same building or close geographical range

- Wide-area networks (WANs): the computers are at a distance and are connected through telephone lines or radio waves

- **Campus-area networks (CANs):** the computers are within a specific, geographic area, such as a school campus or military base

- **Metropolitan-area networks (MANs):** a data network developed for a specific town or city

- **Home-area networks (HANs):** a network contained within a private home which connects all the digital devices

- **Internet:** the largest network in the world, comprised of devises communicating and sharing data via shared routers and servers using common protocols

Depending on the type of network access, the teacher has the productivity tools, instructional information, and communications capabilities that range from the next office to around the world.

Sample Test Questions and Rationale

(Average)

1. **Describe the difference between a LAN and a WAN?**

    A. LANs allow computers to communicate over greater distances than LANs

    B. LANs allow computers to communicate over greater distances than WANs

    C. WANs and LANs provide the same geographical range

    D. WANs and LANs are both ineffective

    The answer is A.

    With Local Area Networks (LANs), the computers are all contained within the same building or close geographical range. Wide Area Networks (WANs) allow computers to communicate over greater distances.

(Easy)

2. **A computer network includes physical infrastructure such as which of the following?**

    A. Software

    B. Web sites

    C. Operating systems

    D. Cables

    The answer is D.

    In part, a computer network includes physical infrastructure like wires, cables, fiber optic lines, undersea cables, and satellites.

COMPETENCY 5
PLANNING INSTRUCTION

> **SKILL Knows techniques for planning instruction, including addressing
> 5.1 curriculum goals, selecting content topics, and incorporating
> learning theory, subject matter, curriculum requirements, and
> student development and interests**

Teaching was once seen as a simple job of developing lesson plans, teaching, going home early, and taking the summer off. However, the demands of a classroom involve much more than grading papers. To begin with, the single task of writing lesson plans is very complicated. **LESSON PLANS** help guide classroom instruction and incorporates the nuts and bolts of a teaching unit. It outlines the steps to both implement the lesson and assess the capacity of the teacher's instruction and the students' learning. Through the lesson plan, teachers identify their objectives and quantify learning goals. They then incorporate effective performance-based assessments to identify when students have learned the material presented.

> **LESSON PLAN:** a plan that outlines the steps to both implement the lesson and assess the capacity of the teacher's instruction and the students' learning

Planning for Classroom Instruction

The effective teacher takes care to select appropriate activities and classroom situations in which learning is optimized. Instructional activities and classroom conditions should be manipulated in a manner that enhances group and individual learning opportunities. For example, the classroom teacher can plan group activities in which students cooperate, share ideas, and discuss topics. In addition to enhancing academic growth, cooperative learning can teach students to collaborate and share personal and cultural ideas and values.

> *The effective teacher takes care to select appropriate activities and classroom situations in which learning is optimized.*

Selecting learning activities

The effective teacher selects learning activities based on specific learning objectives. Ideally, teachers should only plan activities that augment the specific objectives of the lesson and reinforce the teacher's presentation. Additionally, selected learning objectives should be consistent with state and district educational goals, which in turn should focus on national educational goals (Goals 2000). Lesson plans should also target the specific strengths and weaknesses of individual students. The effective teacher plans his/her learning activities to introduce them in a meaningful instructional sequence with relevant activities reinforcing instruction.

Compiling a lesson plan

The purpose of every lesson should be to increase student learning. To ascertain whether there has been student learning and effective teaching, all components of a lesson plan must be present. These include the unit description, learning targets, learning experiences, rationale, and assessments. Together, these can provide both quantitative and qualitative data on attainment of national and state learning standards.

The teacher, the students, and the school will all be measured by the students' scores at the end of the year. So, not only must the teacher be knowledgeable about state and local standards, he or she must structure classes in ways that will meet those frameworks.

Identifying objects/goals

Behavioral objectives must include state and local expectations. They must also be measurable so that when the unit or semester is complete, it is clear whether students have accomplished what was expected. Once goals and objectives have been identified and established, it is important to ensure that they match students' abilities and needs. This will keep some objectives from being too basic for higher-level students, while others are above some students' current level of knowledge.

Evaluating student needs

There are many ways to evaluate student needs and to ensure that all goals are challenging yet achievable. Teachers should check a student's reading level and prior subject area achievement. This information is usually in the cumulative file, located in the guidance office or the main office. This provides a basis for goal setting but shouldn't be the only method used. Depending on the subject area, some other methods that could be useful in determining if all goals are appropriate include:

- Basic skills tests
- Reading level evaluations
- Writing samples
- Interest surveys

In addition to these methods, informal observations should always be used. Finally, a student's level of motivation must also be considered when addressing student needs.

Teachers must plan for the day, the week, the unit, the semester, and the year. The subject matter must be age-appropriate, relevant to students' lives, and in their realm of anticipated interest. The teacher must ask deliberate questions to formulate a plan. For example, should politically controversial issues be introduced or avoided? These decisions can be made on the basis of feedback from students while also keeping sight of the objectives.

Modifying objectives

When given objectives by the school or county, teachers may wish to adapt them so that they can meet the needs of their student population. For example, if a high-level advanced class is given the objective "State five causes of World War II," a teacher may wish to adapt the objective to a higher level, such as "State five causes of World War II and explain how they contributed to the start of the war." Subsequently, objectives can be modified for a lower level as well: "From a list of causes, pick three that specifically caused World War II."

Organizing objectives

When organizing and sequencing objectives, remember that skills are building blocks. Using a **TAXONOMY** of educational objectives can be helpful. The lowest level on the taxonomy is knowledge of material. Therefore, this should be emphasized early in the sequence. For example, memorizing definitions or memorizing famous quotes should be the first part of a lesson. Eventually, objectives should be developed to include higher-level thinking such as:

- Comprehension: being able to use a definition
- Application: being able to apply the definition to other situations
- Synthesis: being able to add other information
- Evaluation: being able to assess the value of something

| **TAXONOMY:** a general term for the organization and classification of information |

Utilizing all the tools

When projects and themes are selected based on the children's interests, this is considered an emergent curriculum. The teacher uses all the tools to assess students at the beginning of and throughout the unit or semester. As the teacher gets to know the learners, he or she listens to their interests and creates a curriculum in response.

WEBBING is a recent concept related to the idea of an emergent curriculum. The two main uses are in planning and recording the curriculum. Planning "webs" are used to generate and record ideas for activities and projects. Activities can be grouped by different areas of the room or by developmental domains. For example, clusters could fall under areas such as dramatic play or science or around domains such as language, cognitive, and physical development. Either configuration works, but being consistent in each web is important. This format will work as a unit, weekly, or monthly program plan. Any new activities that emerge throughout the unit can also be added to the web. The record from the student's ideas will help plan future activities.

| **WEBBING:** a tool used in the planning and recording of curriculum |

Sample Test Questions and Rationale

(Average)

1. **What would improve planning for instruction?**

   A. Describing the role of the teacher and student

   B. Assessing the outcomes of prior instruction

   C. Rearranging the order of activities

   D. Giving outside assignments

The answer is B.

It is important to plan the content, materials, activities, and goals of a lesson. However, these steps will not make a difference if students are not able to demonstrate improvement in the skills being taught. Planning frequently misses the mark or fails to allow for unexpected factors. The teacher must constantly adapt all aspects of the curriculum to what is actually happening in the classroom. Effective instruction occurs when the teacher assesses the outcomes regularly and then makes adjustments accordingly.

(Rigorous)

2. **Teachers must use lesson plans to do all of the following except:**

   A. Meet specified goals and objectives

   B. Match the lesson to students' abilities and needs

   C. Test a strategy proposed by a research journal

   D. Meet state and local learning standards

The answer is C.

Lesson plans must meet specified goals and objectives, it is important to ensure that they match students' abilities and needs. In addition, the lesson's objectives must include state and local expectations.

SKILL 5.2 Knows techniques for creating effective bridges between curriculum goals and students' experiences

Prior Knowledge of Students

Students are not blank slates. They bring the knowledge they have already accumulated regarding their worlds and the people in them. These come from their parents' and the students themselves, and are unique to each child. Getting to know the students well enough to understand some of those preconceptions will make for a more successful year. In essence, the teacher is slowing building on knowledge or adding knowledge to what students already know. Cognitively, this makes a great deal of sense. Think of a file cabinet. When we already have files for certain things, it is easy for us to find a file and put new information into it. When we are given something that does not fit into one of the preexisting files, we struggle to know what to do with it. The same is true with human minds.

Utilizing students' prior knowledge

It is a wise teacher who uses students' prior knowledge as a resource in classroom planning and management. In teaching new skills, guided practice uses students' prior knowledge, which allows students to accept and incorporate new concepts. For example, if younger students are learning to use the computer to access certain information, the teacher can use guided practice to help them develop their skills and understanding of what the computer offers.

Getting Students Involved

Two powerful internal factors influencing students' academic focus and success are their attitudes and perceptions about learning. When instructional objectives center on students' interests and are relevant to their lives, effective learning occurs.

Learners must believe that assigned tasks have some value and that they have the ability and resources to perform them. If a student thinks a task is unimportant, he or she will not put much effort into it. If a student thinks he or she lacks the ability or resources to successfully complete a task, even attempting the task becomes too great a risk. Not only must the teacher understand the students' abilities and interests, he or she must also help students develop positive attitudes and perceptions about learning and associated tasks.

Importance of teacher enthusiasm

Despite a teacher's best efforts to provide important and appropriate instruction, there may be times when a concept, skill, or topic may seem trivial and irrelevant to students. These tasks can be effectively presented if the teacher exhibits a sense of enthusiasm and excitement about the content. Teachers can help spark the students' interest by providing anecdotes and interesting digressions. Research indicates that as teachers become significantly more enthusiastic, students exhibit increased on-task behavior.

If students are to become critical thinkers, they must also be wise explorers. The more they are successful at solving problems, the more they will become confident and willing to explore and claim responsibility for their own thoughts, ideas, and conclusions. Teachers should foster this growth in students of every age.

Sample Test Question and Rationale

(Rigorous)

1. Two powerful internal factors influencing students' academic focus and success are their _____ and _____.

   A. resources and class sizes

   B. parental involvement and teacher preparation

   C. efforts and academic outcomes

   D. attitudes and perceptions about learning

The answer is D.

Students' attitudes and perceptions about learning are two powerful factors influencing academic focus and success. Learners must believe that assigned tasks have some value and that they have the ability and resources to perform them. If a student thinks a task is unimportant, he or she will not put much effort into it.

COMPETENCY 6
ASSESSMENT STRATEGIES

SKILL 6.1 Knows types and characteristics of various assessments

In evaluating school reform efforts, students' performance measures must be assessed. These performance indicators are operationalized through the learning activities planned by the teacher. At varying stages of instruction, the intended outcome must be measured, the level of goal attainment established, and this continuous cycle of student evaluation proceeds. Many forms of assessments are objective, such as multiple choice, yes/no, true/false, and matching. Essays and portfolios, on the other hand, are considered open-ended and allow students to provide answers that are more authentic.

Assessments

The assessment of students is a very important aspect of the teaching and learning process. Periodic testing measures learning outcomes based on established objectives. It also provides information at various stages of learning to determine future student needs such as periodic reviews, reteaching, and enrichment. Educators may implement and assess student academic performance using norm-referenced, criterion-referenced, and performance-based assessments.

Norm-referenced assessments

Standardized achievement tests can be norm-referenced or criterion-reference. In NORM-REFERENCED MEASUREMENTS the performance of the student is compared with the performance of other students who also took the same test. The original group of students who took the test establishes the norm. Norms can be based on age, sex, grade level, geographical location, ethnicity, or other broad classifications.

Standardized, norm-referenced achievement tests are designed to measure what a student knows in a particular subject in relation to other students of similar characteristics. The test batteries provide a broad scope of content area coverage so that it may be used on a larger scale in many different states and school districts. However, the questions may not measure the goals and content emphasized in a particular local curriculum. Therefore, using standardized tests to assess the success of the curriculum or teachers' effectiveness should be avoided (McMillan, 1997).

Uses of norm-referenced scores

Norm-referenced, standardized achievement tests produce different types of scores that are useful in different ways. The most common types of scores are the percentile ranks or percentile scores, grade equivalent scores, stanines, and percentage of items answered correctly.

Percentile scores

The PERCENTILE SCORE indicates how the students' performance compares to the norming group. It tells what percentage of the norming group was outscored by a particular student taking the test. For example, a student scoring at the eightieth percentile did better than eighty percent of the students in the norming group. Likewise, twenty percent of the norming group scored above the particular student, and eighty percent scored below. The scores are indicative of relative strengths and weaknesses. A student may show consistent strengths in language arts and consistent weakness in mathematics as indicated by the scores derived from the test. Yet one could not base remediation solely on these conclusions without a closer item analysis or a closer review of the objectives measured by the test.

> Educators may implement and assess student academic performance using norm-referenced, criterion-referenced, and performance-based assessments.

> **NORM-REFERENCED MEASUREMENTS:** analyze how a student's performance compares to that of other students who took a test

> **PERCENTILE SCORE:** indicates how the students' performance compares to the norming group

Grade equivalency score

The **GRADE EQUIVALENCY SCORE** is expressed by year and month in school for each student. It is used to measure growth and progress. It indicates where a student stands in reference to the norming group. For example, a second-grade student who obtained a grade equivalent score of 4.5 on the language arts section of the test is really not achieving at the fourth grade five month level as one may think. The 4.5 grade equivalence means that the second grader has achieved at about the same level of the norming group who is in the fifth month of the fourth grade, if indeed such a student did take the test. However, when compared to other second graders in the norming group, the student may be about average.

A point of consideration with grade equivalence is that one may never know how well the second grader might do if placed in the fourth grade or how poorly the second grader might do if given the fourth grade test compared to other second graders in the norming group.

Stanines

STANINES indicate where the score is located on the normal curve for the norming group. Stanines are statistically determined but are not as precise as percentile ranking because it only gives the area in which the score is located, but not the precise location. Using stanines to report standard scores is still found to be practical and easy to understand for many parents and school personnel. Stanines range from one to nine (1–9) with five being the middle of the distribution.

Percentage of items answered correctly

Finally, achievement test scores can be reported by percentage of items answered correctly. This form of reporting may not be very meaningful when there are only a few questions/items in a particular category. This makes it difficult to determine if the student guessed well at the items, was just lucky at selecting the right answers, or knowingly chose the correct responses.

Criterion-referenced assessments

CRITERION-REFERENCED ASSESSMENTS (or standardized achievement tests) are designed to indicate the student's performance that is directly related to specific educational objectives, thus indicating what the student can or cannot do. For example, the test may measure how well a student can subtract by regrouping in the tens place or how well a student can identify the long vowel sound in specific words.

Criterion-referenced tests are specific to a particular curriculum, which allows the determination of the effectiveness of the curriculum, as well as specific skills acquired by the students. They also provide information needed to plan for future student needs. Because of the recognized value of criterion-referenced standardized achievement tests, many publishers have developed tailor-made tests

GRADE EQUIVALENCY SCORE: this score indicates where a student stands in reference to the norming group

STANINES: indicate where the score is located on the normal curve for the norming group

CRITERION-REFERENCED ASSESSMENTS: these assessments are designed to indicate the student's performance that is directly related to specific educational objectives, thus indicating what the student can or cannot do

to correlate with state and districts' general goals and specific learning objectives by pulling from a test bank of field-tested items. The test scores are reported by percentage of items answered correctly to indicate mastery or non-mastery.

Performance-based assessments

PERFORMANCE-BASED ASSESSMENTS are currently being used in a number of state testing programs to measure the learning outcomes of individual students in subject content areas. For example, to measure student-learning performance, Washington State uses the Washington Assessment of Student Learning (WASL) in Reading, Writing, Math and Science. This assessment became a high-stakes test when, for the class of 2008, passing it became a graduation requirement.

In today's classrooms, performance-based assessments in core subject areas must be monitored systematically. The process must include pretesting and daily or weekly gauging of student learning. Typical performance assessments include oral and written student work, which can take the form of:

- Research papers

- Oral presentations

- Class projects

- Journals

- Portfolios

- Community service projects

If they are effective, performance assessments will show the gaps or holes that can be then be filled through careful planning.

> **PERFORMANCE-BASED ASSESSMENTS:** these assessments measure the learning outcomes of individual students in subject content areas

Summary

With today's emphasis on student learning accountability, the public and legislature demand effective teaching. Thus, assessment of student learning will remain a mandate in educational accountability. Each method, norm-referenced, criterion-referenced, and performance-based assessments, has costs and benefits. Before a state, district, or school community can determine which type of testing is the most effective, they must determine how the assessment will meet the learning goals and objectives of the students.

Sample Test Questions and Rationale

(Easy)

1. **Which of the following test items is not objective?**

   A. Multiple choice

   B. Essay

   C. Matching

   D. True/false

The answer is B.

Many forms of assessments are objective, such as multiple choice, yes/no, true/false, and matching. Essays and portfolios on the other hand, are considered open-ended and allow students to provide answers that are more authentic.

(Rigorous)

2. **Of the following definitions, which best describes a standardized achievement test?**

   A. It measures narrow skills and abilities

   B. It measures broad areas of knowledge

   C. It measures the ability to perform a task

   D. It measures performance related to specific, recently acquired information

The answer is B.

Standardized achievement tests measure a broad scope of content area knowledge. In this way it may be used on a larger scale in many different states and school districts.

(Rigorous)

3. **Norm-referenced tests:**

   A. Provide information about how local test takers performed compared to local test takers from the previous year

   B. Provide information about how the local test takers performed compared to a representative sampling of national test takers

   C. Make no comparisons to national test takers

   D. None of the above

The answer is B.

Norm-referenced tests are designed to measure what a student knows in a particular subject in relation to other students of similar characteristics. They typically provide information about how the local test takers did compared to a representative sampling of national test takers.

Sample Test Questions and Rationale (cont.)

(Average)

4. It is most appropriate to use norm-referenced standardized tests for which of the following?

    A. For comparison to the population on which the test was normed

    B. For teacher evaluation

    C. For evaluation of the administration

    D. For comparison to school on which the test was normed

The answer is A.

While the efficacy of norm-referenced standardized tests have come under attack recently, they are currently the best device for determining where an individual student stands compared to a wide range of peers. They also provide a measure for a program or a school to evaluate how their own students are doing as compared to the populace at large. Even so, they should not be the only measure upon which decisions are made or evaluations drawn. There are many other instruments for measuring student achievement that the teacher needs to consult and take into account.

(Rigorous)

5. _____ is a standardized test in which performance is directly related to the educational objective(s)

    A. Aptitude test

    B. Norm-referenced test

    C. Criterion-referenced test

    D. Summative evaluation

The answer is C.

A criterion-referenced test takes the educational objectives of a course and rewrites them in the form of questions. The questions on the test are directly related to the objectives upon which the instruction is based. Thus the results of a criterion-referenced test will tell which objectives of the course a student has mastered and which one he or she has not mastered.

SKILL 6.2 Knows uses for assessments

Purposes and Uses of Assessment

There are seven purposes of assessment:

1. To assist student learning

2. To identify students' strengths and weaknesses

3. To assess the effectiveness of a particular instructional strategy

4. To assess and improve the effectiveness of curriculum programs

5. To assess and improve teaching effectiveness

6. To provide data that assists in decision making

7. To communicate with and involve parents and other stakeholders

In a general sense, assessments can take four forms:

1. Observation: noticing someone and judging their actions.

2. Informal continuous assessment: not formal like a test or exam. It is continuous because it occurs periodically, such as on a daily or weekly basis.

3. Formal continuous assessment: more structured activity organized to measure learners progress, such as quizzes or group activities.

4. Formal assessment: structured infrequent measure of learner achievement, such as tests and exams.

INFORMAL ASSESSMENT: a type of assessment that is more casual and not highly structured

FORMAL ASSESSMENT: a type of assessment that is highly structured and usually graded or scored to evaluate student performance; these can be both continuous or periodic

INFORMAL ASSESSMENTS help teachers measure how well the learners are processing information and progressing. Informal assessments can be in the form of homework assignments, field journals, and daily class work. Teachers then use the information gathered to tailor instruction to student needs.

On the other hand, FORMAL ASSESSMENTS are highly structured. They are conducted at regular intervals and if the progress is not satisfactory, interventions, including parent involvement, are absolutely essential. Tests, exams, and projects are types of formal assessments.

Classification of Assessments

Assessments can be classified as follows:

- Diagnostic assessments: determine individual strengths and weaknesses in specific areas.

- Readiness assessments: measure prerequisite knowledge and skills.

- Interest and Attitude assessments: attempt to identify topics of high interest or areas in which students may need extra motivational support.

- Evaluation assessments: generally program- or teacher-focused.

- Placement assessments: used for grouping students or determining where each student should begin in leveled materials.

- Formative assessments: provide ongoing feedback on student progress and the effectiveness of instructional methods and materials.

- Summative assessments: determine the degree of student mastery or learning that has taken place. Usually a value, such as a grade, is placed on the student's performance.

It is important to remember that in education, the main purpose of evaluation is to guide instruction. Therefore, tests must measure not only what a student has learned, but also what a student has yet to learn and what a teacher must teach. Although today's educators utilize many forms of assessment, testing remains an integral part of instruction and evaluation.

Sample Test Questions and Rationale

(Rigorous)

1. **Which of the following is the least appropriate reason for teachers to be able to analyze data on their students?**

   A. To provide appropriate instruction

   B. To make instructional decisions

   C. To separate students into weaker and stronger academic groups

   D. To communicate and determine instructional progress

The answer is C.

Especially in today's high stakes environment, it is critical teachers have a complete understanding of the process involved in examining student data in order to make instructional decisions, prepare lessons, determine progress, and report progress to stakeholders.

Sample Test Questions and Rationale (cont.)

(Easy)

2. The seven purposes of assessment include all of the following except:

    A. To identify students' strengths and weaknesses

    B. To assess the effectiveness of a particular instructional strategy

    C. To provide data that assists in decision making

    D. None of the above

The answer is D.

The seven purposes of assessment are:

- To assist student learning

- To identify students' strengths and weaknesses

- To assess the effectiveness of a particular instructional strategy

- To assess and improve the effectiveness of curriculum programs

- To assess and improve teaching effectiveness

- To provide data that assists in decision making

- To communicate with and involve parents and other stakeholders

(Average)

3. What is the best example of a formative assessment?

    A. The results of an intelligence test

    B. Correcting tests in small groups and immediately recording the grades

    C. An essay that receives teacher feedback and can be corrected by students prior to having a grade recorded

    D. Scheduling a discussion prior to the test

The answer is C.

Formative assessments provide ongoing feedback on student progress and the effectiveness of instructional methods and materials. An example is an essay that receives teacher feedback and that can be corrected by students prior to having a grade recorded.

Accuracy in Student Evaluation

The accuracy of student evaluation is essential. ACCURACY is determined by the usability of the instrument and the consistency of measurement, which is observed through reliability and validity of the instruments.

VALIDITY is the extent to which a test measures what it is intended to measure. For example, a test may lack validity if it was designed to measure the creative writing of students, but it is also used to measure handwriting even though it was not designed for the latter.

RELIABILITY refers to the consistency of the test to measure what it should measure. For example, the items on a true or false quiz, given by a classroom teacher, are reliable if they convey the same meaning every time the quiz is administered to similar groups of students under similar situations. In other words, there is no ambiguity or confusion with the items on the quiz.

Difference between reliability and validity

The difference between validity and reliability can be visualized as throwing darts at a dartboard. There is validity if the dart hits the target (an assessment measures what it is intended to measure), it is reliable if the same spot is hit time after time (the assessment consistently measures what it should measure). The goal should be to develop assessments that are both valid and reliable (every time the assessment is administered, it measures what it is intended to measure).

> **ACCURACY:** this is the usability of the instrument and the consistency of a measurement, which is observed through reliability and validity of the instruments

> **VALIDITY:** the extent to which a test measures what it is intended to measure

> **RELIABILITY:** the consistency of the test to measure what it should measure

Reliability versus Validity

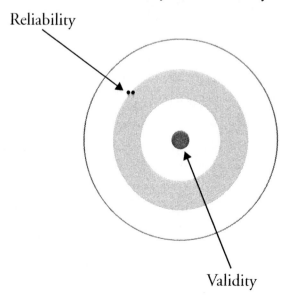

Reliability

Validity

A perfect positive correlation equals + 1.00 and a perfect negative correlation equals -1.00. The reliability of an assessment tool is generally expressed as a decimal to two places (e.g., 0.85). This decimal describes the correlation that would be expected between two scores if the same student took the test repeatedly.

Determining reliability

There are several ways to estimate the reliability of an instrument. The simplest approach is the TEST-RETEST METHOD. When the same test is administered again to the same students, if the test is perfectly reliable, each student will receive the same score each time. Even as the scores of individual students vary slightly from one time to the next, it is desirable for the rank order of the students to remain unchanged.

Other methods of estimating reliability rely on the same conceptual framework. SPLIT-HALF METHODS divide a single test into two parts and compare them. EQUIVALENT FORMS METHODS compare two versions of the same test. With some types of assessment, such as essays and observation reports, reliability also deals with the procedures and criteria used for scoring. The inter-rater reliability asks the question: How much will the results vary depending on who is scoring or rating the assessment data?

Determining validity

There are three common types of validity:

1. Content validity: describes the degree to which a test actually tests what it sets out to test. For example, in mathematics, a complex story problem will lower the validity of an arithmetic test because the story problem allows a student's reading ability to affect the results. However, note that it remains a valid test of the student's ability to solve story problems.

2. Criterion validity: deals with the test's ability to predict performance on another measure or test. For example, a college admissions test has high criterion validity if it accurately predicts those students who will attain high GPAs at a particular college. The criterion in this case is college GPA.

3. Construct validity: shows how well an assessment measures a particular theoretical concept such as intelligence or creativity. For example, intelligence is an idea or concept that is defined in many ways; therefore, an IQ test may have construct validity for someone who defines intelligence according to IQ. Conversely, someone who believes in multiple intelligences may say that an IQ test lacks construct validity. In either case, the validity is determined according to the definitions and dimensions of the construct being measured. First, the construct must be properly defined, then the assessment can be judged to see if it measures the construct in a valid way.

TEST-RETEST METHOD: a method of detemining reliability when the same test is administered again to the same students to ensure that the same scores are received

SPLIT-HALF METHOD: a method of comparing two versions of the same test

EQUIVALENT FORMS METHOD: a method of dividing a single test into two parts and comparing them

Sample Test Questions and Rationale

(Rigorous)

1. Fill in the blanks for I. _____ and II. _____ in the picture below:

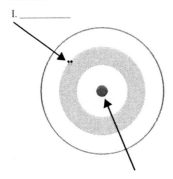

I. _____

A. I. Reliability and II. Validity

B. I. Validity and II. Reliability

C. I. Reliability and II. Vigor

D. I. Rigor and II. Validity

The answer is A.

This picture represents I. Reliability and II. Validity.

(Easy)

2. This method tests the validity and reliability of a test by dividing a single test into two parts and comparing them.

A. Split-half

B. Test-retest

C. Equivalent forms

D. Two-set

The answer is A.

There are several ways to estimate the reliability of an instrument. The simplest approach is the test-retest method. When the same test is administered again to the same students, if the test is perfectly reliable, each student will receive the same score each time. Even as the scores of individual students vary slightly from one time to the next, it is desirable for the rank order of the students to remain unchanged. Other methods of estimating reliability rely on the same conceptual framework. Split-half methods divide a single test into two parts and compare them. Equivalent forms methods compare two versions of the same test.

(Average)

3. An example of reliability in testing is _____.

A. items on the test produce the same response each time

B. the test was administered with poor lighting

C. items on the test measure what they should measure

D. the test is too long for the time allotted

The answer is A.

When a test is reliable, it produces the same response each time. A test should give the same results when administered under the same conditions and to the same types of groups of students. This occurs when the items on the test are clear, unambiguous, and not confusing for the students. When items on the test measure what they should measure, this is called validity.

SKILL Interprets and communicates results of assessments

The teacher appreciates the importance of knowing and understanding students in order to provide the most effective learning opportunities. Therefore, the teacher is aware of and uses a variety of strategies for developing this knowledge of students' strengths and weaknesses. In addition he or she is able to share this knowledge with the students, their parents, and others.

Tests

Tests are essential for the learner in understanding his/her current achievements and learning difficulties. Tests can have strong consequences for students, therefore, they should not be taken lightly, nor should they be given haphazardly. No longer can a teacher rely on ready-made tests to precisely assess what students know. To obtain an accurate measure of student progress, the teacher must know how to plan and construct tests. In addition, the teacher must know how to:

- Administer tests

- Arm students with test-taking skills

- Provide feedback on test performance

Research indicates that students do their best when they are motivated and aware of and able to apply test-taking skills. In addition, teachers must use test data as a meaningful aspect of instruction. For instance, it can be used to increase student motivation, especially when this information is available in the form of feedback. Using this strategy, teachers frequently administer tests and give immediate feedback, which is an effective way to increase achievement.

Standardized testing

Standardized testing is currently under great scrutiny; however, educators agree that all tests have a purpose. Each type serves as a means of gathering information about student's learning and most can provide accurate, helpful data for improving instruction. Notwithstanding, formative assessments should be the most common types administered. These are the basic, everyday types of assessments teachers continually use to understand students' growth and to help them achieve.

Observations

Valuable information can be obtained through teacher observations. Teachers are constantly observing students and making assessments about their performance, which in turn influences future instruction. **INFORMAL OBSERVATIONS** allow teachers to observe students with no predetermined focus. Through such observations, teachers may identify students who can work independently versus those who require a great deal of guidance. Informal observations can lead to more formal assessments, which can then lead to serious interventions and/or parent conferences.

Global and behavioral observations

A **GLOBAL OBSERVATION** is a teacher's written account of a student's: interaction with peers, general attitude toward school and learning, overall ability to satisfactorily complete assignments, and typical behavior. It is written in lay terms without educational jargon and is therefore easily understood by parents. This document contains pertinent information about a student's class performance and is a valuable tool for school administrators, guidance counselors, psychologists, and other personnel who may be involved with the student.

A **BEHAVIORAL OBSERVATION** is a written anecdotal record of a student's behavior and activities for a specific period of time. The teacher records both the beginning and ending times for the observation and precisely indicates the student's every movement, utterance, and action during that designated time. This type of observation is valuable in determining a student's activity level and ability to attend to prescribed tasks.

Formal observations

Occasionally more **FORMAL OBSERVATIONS** are needed. In these cases, there is a specified focus, and predetermined, sample behavior is systematically observed. This is done because some goals or objectives can only be assessed by observation, such as those that occur during cooperative group activities. Formal observations often allow teachers to benefit from new information that may challenge some of their opinions about students.

Formal observations can be included in a student's record, as they add to the history of a student's education. Meaningful information such as the student's attendance, grade averages, and general health are also a part of the record. Some basic information about the student's family, current address, and schools attended is included. Standardized test scores and dates of administration are also an important aspect of the student's record.

The narrative is a written record, which may be contained within a student's cumulative record. Teachers can use this information to set goals for individual students or to structure future activities. The information acquired through any of these tools can best be reported through a parent/student conference or

INFORMAL OBSERVATION: allows teachers to observe students with no predetermined focus

GLOBAL OBSERVATION: a teacher's written account of a student's: interaction with peers, general attitude toward school and learning, overall ability to satisfactorily complete assignments, and typical behavior

BEHAVIORAL OBSERVATION: a written anecdotal record of a student's behavior and activities for a specific period of time

FORMAL OBSERVATION: an observation where there is a specified focus, and pre-determined, sample behavior is systematically observed

a meeting with other educators. Although written reports could summarize the knowledge the teacher has gained, a more thorough explanation can be presented through a face-to-face meeting.

Student Records

STUDENTS' RECORDS:
a collection of documents about a certain student, including test scores and observations, that help an educator get a more accurate feel for a student's needs

The information contained within STUDENTS' RECORDS, teacher observations, and diagnostic tests are only as valuable as the teacher's ability to understand them. Although these data are contained in the student's cumulative record, it is the responsibility of each teacher to read and interpret the information.

Student test results

Diagnostic test results are somewhat uniform and easy to interpret. They usually include a scoring guide that tells the teacher what the numbers actually mean. Teachers also need to realize that these scores are not the ultimate indicator of a student's ability or learning needs. Many factors influence these scores including:

- How the student regarded the value or importance of the test

- How the student was feeling when the test was administered

- The rapport the student had with the tester

Therefore, the teacher should regard these scores as a "ball park" figure.

Interpreting other teachers' observations

When a teacher reads another teacher's observations, it is important to keep in mind that each person brings certain biases to an observation. The reader may also influence the information contained within an observation with his/her own interpretation. It is necessary to be aware of these shortcomings when using teacher observations as a basis for designing learning programs.

Student records may provide the most assistance in guiding instruction. These records contain information that was gathered over a period of time and may show student growth and progress. They also hold information provided by several people including teachers, parents, and other educators or professionals. By reading this compilation of information, the teacher may get a more accurate feel for a student's needs, how he or she learns, what he or she knows, and what he or she needs to know to further his/her education.

Communicating Results

In addition to interpreting the results of ongoing assessments, it is also the teacher's job to communicate these results with the student's parents and future teachers. Just as the current teacher uses prior information to make instructional decisions, future teachers will also rely on the current teacher's records. Also, teachers should make themselves available if a future teacher needs clarification on a student's issue(s). Lastly, the teacher must ensure that parents receive the results of all assessments, and that they understand the results completely. Often, this can be accomplished through:

- Phone calls

- Letters

- Short meetings

- Special parent/teacher conferences

DOMAIN III
COMMUNICATION TECHNIQUES

PERSONALIZED STUDY PLAN

KNOWN MATERIAL/ SKIP IT

COMPETENCY 7
EFFECTIVE COMMUNICATION TECHNIQUES

SKILL **Knows basic, effective verbal and non-verbal communication**
7.1 **techniques**

Student Age and Communication

Effective teachers are well versed in cognitive development, which is crucial to presenting ideas and or materials to students at a level appropriate to their developmental maturity. These educators also have the ability to use nonverbal and verbal patterns of communications that focus on age-appropriate instructions and materials.

Consistent with Piaget's theory of cognitive development, younger children (below age eight) have limited language skills. In contrast, older children (age eight through high school) are capable of solving complex problems. These students, naturally, should have more detailed instructions and materials that require more advanced language skills.

Communication in the Classroom

The classroom environment has become an increasing milieu of cognitive, social, emotional, and cultural diversity. The effective teacher must rise to the challenge of presenting ideas and materials appropriate for varying levels of students, while still being relevant to students as a whole. Research indicates that successful teachers first, ensure that assignments are understood and second, hold students responsible for assignments. The clearer the students' understanding of the objectives, the more effective instruction will be. Therefore, teachers must identify and articulate the specific behaviors that are expected during and after the completion of tasks.

Implementing successful communication

Learning will be increased if the teacher begins a lesson by providing orientation and direction, such as stating the objectives and outlining the lesson content. Besides telling the students what they are going to learn, teachers may choose to use advance organizers that include visual motivations such as:

Effective teachers are well versed in cognitive development, which is crucial to presenting ideas and or materials to students at a level appropriate to their developmental maturity.

- Outlines

- Graphs

- Models

J. M. Kallison, Jr. found that subject matter retention increased when lessons included an outline at the beginning of the lesson and a summary at the end. This type of structure is utilized in successful classrooms and is especially valuable to the visual learner and is a motivational factor for most students. Next, he or she must support the lesson's momentum by providing distinct explanations. The instructor must:

- Effectively transition from one part of the lesson to another

- Check for student comprehension

- Provide practice where it is appropriate

Specific questions asked at the beginning of a lesson can also help students focus on the content and be more attentive to instruction. Effective teachers also clearly explain difficult points during a lesson and then analyze problems utilizing questioning techniques with the students.

Sample Test Questions and Rationale

(Easy)

1. Outlines, graphs, and models are particularly good for which type of learners?

   A. Auditory

   B. Kinestetic

   C. Visual

   D. Olfactory

The answer is C.

Teachers may choose to use advance organizers that include outlines, graphs, and models. This practice is especially valuable to the visual learner and is a motivational factor for most students.

(Average)

2. What has research shown to be the effect of using advance organizers in the lesson?

   A. They facilitate learning and retention

   B. They allow teachers to use their planning time effectively

   C. They only serve to help the teacher organize the lesson

   D. They show definitive positive results on student achievement

The answer is A.

J.M. Kallison, Jr. found that subject matter retention increased when lessons included an outline at the beginning of the lesson and a summary at the end. This type of structure is utilized in successful classrooms and is especially valuable to the visual learner and is a motivational factor for most students.

COMPETENCY 8
EFFECTS ON CLASSROOM COMMUNICATION

SKILL **Knows effect of cultural and gender differences on**
8.1 **communications in the classroom**

To create an effective learning culture, there must be a positive environment that facilitates discussion-oriented, nonthreatening communication among all students. The teacher must take the lead and model appropriate actions and speech, and intervene quickly when a student makes a misstep and offends another (this often happens inadvertently).

Possible Communication Issues

In a diverse classroom, the teacher should be aware of the following communication issues:

- Be sensitive to terminology and language patterns that may exclude or demean students. Regularly switch between the use of "he" and "she" in speech and writing. Know and use the current terms that ethnic and cultural groups use to identify themselves (e.g., "Latinos" [favored] vs. "Hispanics").

- Be aware of body language that is intimidating or offensive to some cultures, such as direct eye contact, and adjust accordingly.

- Monitor your own reactions to students to ensure equal responses to males and females, as well as differently performing students.

- Don't protect students from criticism because of their ethnicity or gender. Likewise, acknowledge and praise all meritorious work without singling out particular students. Both actions can make all students hyper-aware of ethnic and gender differences and cause anxiety or resentment throughout the class.

- Emphasize the importance of discussing and considering different viewpoints and opinions. Demonstrate and express value for all opinions and comments and lead students to do the same.

Student Differences

When teaching in diverse classrooms, teachers must also expect to be working and communicating with students who are diverse. Even without the typical classifications, each student is unique and this should be treated as an asset.

Gender

Another obvious difference among students is gender. Interactions with male students are typically viewed as being different from those with female students. Depending on the lesson, female students may be more interested in working with partners or perhaps even individually. On the other hand, male students may enjoy a more collaborative or hands-on activity. The gender of the teacher will also come into play, particularly with students of a different gender. Of course, every student is different and may not fit into a stereotypical role, and getting to know their students' preferences for learning will help teachers to truly enhance learning in the classroom.

Culture

Most class rosters will also consist of students from a variety of cultures. Teachers should get to know their learners (of all cultures) so that they may incorporate elements of the students' cultures into classroom activities and planning. Getting to know about their backgrounds and cultural traditions helps to build rapport with each student. This also educates the teacher about the world in which he or she teaches.

Language

For students still learning English, teachers must make every attempt to communicate with these learners daily. Whether it is through translation by another student who speaks the same language, word cards, computer programs, drawings, or other methods, teachers must find ways to encourage each student's participation. Of course, the teacher must also be sure the appropriate language services begin for the student in a timely manner.

Socioeconomic backgrounds

SOCIOECONOMIC BACKGROUND: the history of the economic and social lives of a student

Another consideration is different SOCIOECONOMIC BACKGROUNDS. Research has shown that all students are equally capable of performing well in the classroom; unfortunately, students from lower socioeconomic backgrounds are faced with a number of challenges to reaching their full potential.

For instance, single parents may be less able to help their children in completing homework consistently. These families may need help formalizing a homework system, or perhaps the student would need more attention on study or test-taking skills. Teachers should encourage these students as much as possible and offer positive reinforcements when they meet or exceed classroom expectations. Educators should also watch these students carefully for signs of malnutrition, fatigue, and other impediments to learning.

Sample Test Questions and Rationale

(Average)

1. To facilitate discussion-oriented, nonthreatening communication among all students, teachers must do which of the following:

   A. Model appropriate behavior

   B. Allow students to express themselves freely

   C. Show students that some views will not be tolerated

   D. Explain that students should not disagree

   The answer is A.

   To facilitate discussion-oriented, nonthreatening communication among all students, teacher must take the lead and model appropriate actions and speech. They must also intervene quickly when a student makes a misstep and offends another (this often happens inadvertently).

(Average)

2. In diverse classrooms, teachers must ensure that they neither protect students from criticism nor praise them because of their ethnicity or gender. Doing either action may result in which of the following outcomes:

   A. Classmates may become anxious or resentful when dealing with the diverse students

   B. Parents will appreciate their child being singled out

   C. The student will be pleased to receive this attention

   D. Other teachers will follow this example

   The answer is A.

   Don't "protect" students from criticism because of their ethnicity or gender. Likewise, acknowledge and praise all meritorious work without singling out particular students. Both actions can make all students hyper-aware of ethnic and gender differences and cause anxiety or resentment throughout the class.

COMPETENCY 9
TYPES OF COMMUNICATION

**SKILL Knows types of communications and interactions that can
9.1 stimulate discussion in different ways for particular purposes**

A Successful Classroom Environment

Trust is an important component in probing for student understanding. Creative questioning, which requires planning ahead, can sometimes reveal what the teacher needs to know. Another strategy is writing exercises that focus not on correctness but on recording the student's thoughts on a topic. Sometimes assuring the student that only the teacher will see what is written is helpful in freeing students to reveal their own thoughts. When a new unit is introduced, the teacher should include vocabulary lessons related to the unit. This can help students find the words they need to talk or write about the topic.

Student responsibility

If a teacher can help students to take responsibility for their own ideas and thoughts, much can be accomplished. This will only be reached in a nonjudgmental environment that doesn't permit criticism of the ideas of others and that accepts any topic for discussion that is in the realm of appropriateness. Success in problem solving boosts students' confidence and makes them more willing to take risks. Therefore, the teacher must provide those opportunities for success.

Students can be taught the skills that lead to recall of facts, and beginning to teach those skills at early grades will result in more successful students. For example, students need to know that experiencing a fact or an idea in several different ways increases the ability to recall it. Also, it will help them to know that experiences that involve more of the senses will result in a multiplication of their recall abilities.

Open-minded approach

A classroom atmosphere that frowns on closed-mindedness and rewards openness to new and different approaches and ideas is powerful in shaping students' attitudes. Some students will come from homes that practice narrow-minded judgmentalism and criticism of differentness, so there will be obstacles. However, the classroom can be powerful in the development of student's future attitudes and philosophies. Even though some students may seem intractable, remember that the experience of participating in a free and open classroom will have an effect in the long run.

Understanding the student experience

If the teacher stays on the cutting edge of student's experience, they will become more curious about learning what they don't know. For instance, their curiosity will be piqued by a lesson on a particular country or tribe they may not even know exists. Various kinds of media can reveal what life is like for people their own age. In such a presentation, positive aspects of the lives of those "other" youth should be included. Perhaps a correspondence with a village could be developed. It is good for students of all socioeconomic levels to know what the rest of the world is like and, in doing so, develop a curiosity to know more.

What about an animal they know little or nothing about? Many television programs, such as those on PBS or Animal Planet channels, could be very useful in such a unit. The meerkat, for instance, is cute, funny, and interesting, and Animal Planet has a series on this animal.

If the teacher stays on the cutting edge of student's experience, they will become more curious about learning what they don't know. For instance, their curiosity will be piqued by a lesson on a particular country or tribe they may not even know exists.

Learning to question

To analyze the world with critical thinking, students need to know enough about valid and invalid reasoning; with this knowledge, they will know how to ask questions. The teacher should present speeches or essays that demonstrate both valid and invalid examples. This can be useful in helping students develop the ability to question the reasoning of others. Second, because these will be published writers or televised speakers, students are able to question ideas that are accepted by some adults and talk about what is wrong in the thinking of those apparently successful communicators.

Results of a Positive Classroom

When classrooms respect all students, regardless of background, this can positively affect the thinking of students who may come from bigoted families. If someone connected to the class is ill or dies, projects to reach out and express concern, even if only in notes, will be a useful practice in the development of a caring and concerned approach to the plight of others. Also, teachers should encourage volunteering with and assisting strangers such as the victims of a hurricane. This will give them the experience of caring for someone who is suffering. This can also be accomplished through trips to nursing homes to take cards or gifts. The recipients are usually grateful, and this touches students.

Sample Test Question and Rationale

(Rigorous)

1. Which of the following is the best strategy to probe for student understanding of a specific topic:

    A. Assigning writing exercises that are graded for correctness

    B. Allowing students to write on any topic

    C. Suggesting that students write in a journal that is checked at the end of the semester

    D. Assigning writing exercises that focus on recording students' thoughts on the topic

The answer is D.

In probing for student understanding of a specific topic, teachers can assign writing exercises that focus not on correctness but on recording students' thoughts on that topic.

DOMAIN IV
PROFESSION AND COMMUNITY

PERSONALIZED STUDY PLAN

KNOWN MATERIAL/ SKIP IT

COMPETENCY 10
THE REFLECTIVE PRACTITIONER

Comprehensive learning communities must include PROFESSIONAL DEVELOP-
MENT OPPORTUNITIES. These improve teacher performance and result in better
instructional practices. In order to promote the vision, mission, and action plans
of school communities, teachers must be given the tools to maximize their performance. They should strive to develop student-centered learning communities that foster the academic capacities and learning outcomes of
all students.

> **PROFESSIONAL DEVELOPMENT OPPORTUNITIES:** events designed to improve teacher performance and result in better instructional practices

Workshops

Professional development is offered at many levels with the most traditional
occurring at school or district WORKSHOPS. These enhance instructional expectations for teachers and can be supplemented and enhanced by more intense,
multiple-day workshops given by national and state educational organizations.
Such initiatives seek to enhance the federal accountability, skill-levels, and professional expertise of teachers.

> *In order to promote the vision, mission, and action plans of school communities, teachers must be given tools to maximize their performance.*

Most workshops on the national and state level provide clock hours that can be
used for licensure renewals, usually required every five years. Typically, 150 clock
hours are needed for a five-year licensure renewal. Thus, teachers must attend
and complete paperwork for diverse workshops that range from one to fifty clock
hours, according to the timeframe of the workshops.

> **WORKSHOPS:** professional development opportunities designed to enhance the federal accountability, skill-levels, and professional expertise of teachers; they can be sponsored at the school, district, state, or federal level

Ways to Expand Professional Development

Research by the National Association of Secondary Principals', "Breaking Ranks
II: Strategies for Leading High School Reform" created the following multiple listing of educational practices needed for expanding the professional development
opportunities for teachers:

- Interdisciplinary instruction between subject areas

- Identification of individual learning styles to maximize student academic
  performance

- Training teachers in understanding and applying multiple assessment formats and implementations in curriculum and instruction

- Looking at multiple methods of classroom management strategies

- Providing teachers with national, federal, state, and district curriculum expectations and performance outcomes

- Identifying the schools' and communities' action plan of student learning objectives and teacher instructional practices

- Helping teachers understand how to use data to impact student learning goals and objectives

- Teaching teachers on how to disaggregate student data in improving instruction and curriculum implementation for student academic equity and access

- Develop leadership opportunities for teachers to become school and district trainers to promote effective learning communities for student achievement and success

Professional networking

People in business are always encouraged to network in order to further their careers. The same can be said for teaching. If English teachers get together, they develop a sense of community and discuss what is going on in their classrooms. Those discussions make the whole much stronger than the parts. Just knowing that someone else is encountering the same difficulties is useful.

But more than that, talking about the problem will very likely suggest a solution that everyone can take back and use in their own classrooms. Also, some teachers will have focused on a problem more than others and may have found solutions that can be useful. Older teachers can often provide comfort, guidance, and ideas from which young teachers can profit. Associations often facilitate these types of conversations. Even if there are not formal opportunities for such networking, it is wise for schools or even individual teachers to develop them and seek them out.

Teachers should belong to at least one association in their own field if for nothing else than to take advantage of the literature that will provide updates on what is going on in the field.

Professional associations

Teachers should belong to at least one association in their own field if for nothing else than to take advantage of the literature that will provide updates on what is going on in the field. If teachers can attend at least one gathering of that association, it is advised. It's easy to become bogged-down and complacent. Getting away and talking to colleagues from other parts of the country help all practitioners, including teachers, to avoid entrenchment. Listening to what is happening in the field is also useful. It is rare that a teacher attends one of these conferences without making changes in the way his or her classroom is conducted.

Summary

In promoting professional development opportunities for teachers that enhance student achievement, the bottom line is that teachers must be given the time to complete workshops at no or minimal costs. School and district budgets must include financial resources to support and encourage teachers to engage in mandatory and optional professional development opportunities that create a "win-win" situation for the educators and for students.

Sample Test Question and Rationale

(Average)

1. **Teachers should network with one another for all of the following reasons except** _____.

   A. to discuss challenges they face in their classrooms

   B. to develop a sense of community

   C. to earn their clock-hours for licensure renewal

   D. to find solutions to difficult problems

The answer is C.

Educators have begun to encourage networking for teachers to get together and develop a sense of community. This also allows teachers to discuss what is going on in their classrooms; often just knowing that someone else is encountering the same difficulties is useful. But more than that, talking about the problem will very likely suggest a solution that everyone can take back and use in their own classrooms. Also, some teachers will have focused on a problem more than others and may have found solutions that can be useful. Older teachers can often provide comfort, guidance, and ideas from which young teachers can profit.

> ### SKILL 10.2 Possesses the ability to read, understand, and apply articles and books about current research, views, ideas and debates, regarding best teaching practices

Staying Current

Good teachers stay on top of what is going on in the field and are constantly looking for ways to improve their teaching. Articles often provide information that can be applied to the reader's classroom practices. Therefore, research-oriented teachers first read an article more than once carefully to make sure they understanding what is being proposed. In addition, they ask questions such as:

- When was the article written?
- Who wrote it?
- What are the author's credentials?
- Are other writers/professionals writing or speaking about the same idea or approach?

Incorporating New Ideas

Next, they conduct their own literature search to see if they can find where the new theory or approach has been tested and what results have been found. In the case of a debate about a particular theory or practice, they take into account what they have found in their own experience. Just because it is written and published doesn't mean it is true, useful, or applicable to every classroom. Only after the idea passes all of these tests, will experienced teachers incorporate, rate, and evaluate it in their own classrooms.

Sample Test Question and Rationale

(Rigorous)

1. Ms. Jones has just read an article on an exciting new instructional strategy; she is considering incorporating this strategy in her classroom. As a research-oriented professional, what should be her next step?

    A. Read textbooks that deal with a wide range of theories

    B. Perform a literature search to see what else has been written on the topic

    C. Talk with other teachers about their opinions

    D. Begin incorporating the strategy with some students in the class

The answer is B.

Good teachers stay on top of what is going on in the field and are constantly looking for ways to improve their teaching. Articles often provide information that can be applied to classroom practices. Research-oriented teachers first read an article more than once carefully to make sure they understanding what is being proposed. Next, they conduct their own literature search to see if they can find where the new theory or approach has been tested and what results have been found. In the case of a debate about a particular theory or practice, they take into account what they have found in their own experience? Just because it is written and published doesn't mean it is true, useful, or applicable to every classroom. Only after the idea passes all of these tests, will experienced teachers incorporate, rate, and evaluate it in their own classrooms.

SKILL 10.3 Ongoing personal reflection on teaching and learning practices as a basis for making professional decisions

Classroom Challenges

Teachers should have the ultimate goal of providing a comprehensive education for all students. This is facilitated by providing a challenging curriculum and setting high expectations for learning. In an ideal classroom, the climate is conducive for teaching and learning. Most classrooms will have a diversity of learners from a multitude of cultural, ethnic, intellectual, socioeconomic, and academically prepared backgrounds. The reality is that teachers are confronted with classrooms that are infused with classroom-management issues and differentiated learners. Some will be completely engaged in the learning process, others will be negatively removed from all aspects of learning, and the rest will fall somewhere in the middle.

Most classrooms will have a diversity of learners from a multitude of cultural, ethnic, intellectual, socioeconomic, and academically prepared backgrounds. The reality is that teachers are confronted with classrooms that are infused with classroom-management issues and differentiated learners.

Obstacles for new teachers

Research has shown that for new teachers entering the profession, the two greatest obstacles are dealing with behavioral issues and reaching students who are minimally engaged in their own learning processes. Therefore, teachers must maintain a plethora of resources to deal with an ever-changing landscape of learners and classroom environments. The educator's primary professional concern will always be for the student and for the development of the student's potential. He or she will therefore strive for professional growth and will seek to exercise the best professional judgment and integrity.

Developed a student-centered environment

In a student-centered learning environment, the goal is to provide the best education, great learning experiences, and avenues for academic success for all students. This is done by first integrating well-known patterns of physical, social, and academic development. Next, learning plans can be individualized based on each student's skill levels and needs. By using pre- and post-assessments, teachers more effectively develop and maximize a student's potential. These assessments provide comprehensive data on the existing skill level of the student. In turn, the teacher uses this data to plan and adapt curriculum to address and grow student skills. Lastly, involve all stakeholders through a community approach to learning. This involved constant communications with the students and parents and has been shown to maximize student learning.

Maintaining professionalism

Educators must also strive to achieve and sustain the highest degree of ethical conduct and professionalism. This includes maintaining the respect and confidence of one's colleagues, students, parents, and other members of the community. The ethical conduct of an educator has undergone extensive scrutiny in today's classrooms. Teachers must adhere to strict rules and regulations to maintain the highest degree of conduct and professionalism in the classroom. Current court cases in Florida have examined ethical violations of teachers engaged in improper communication and abuse with students, along with teachers engaged in drug violations and substance abuse in classrooms. It is imperative that today's teachers have the highest regard for professionalism and behave as proper role models for students in and out of the classrooms.

Avoiding complacency

The very nature of the teaching profession—the yearly cycle of doing the same thing over and over again—creates the tendency to fossilize, to quit growing, to become complacent. The teachers who are truly successful are those who have built their own safeguards against that. They see themselves as constant learners. They believe that learning never ends. They are careful never to teach their classes the same way each year. They have a tendency to reflect on what is happening to their students or what happened this year as compared to last year. Some questions that a teacher could ask of their methods might be:

- What worked the best?

- What didn't work so well?

- What can be changed to improve success rates?

- What about continuing education?

- Should they go for another degree or should they enroll in more classes?

Effective teachers are constantly reflecting on their teaching and on themselves as learners.

Self-assessment

There are several avenues a teacher might take in order to assess his or her own teaching strengths and weaknesses. If a teacher has several students who do not understand a concept, this is an early indicator that a self-evaluation might be necessary. In such a case, a teacher might want to review his or her lesson plans to make sure the topic is being covered thoroughly and in a clear fashion. Brainstorming other ways to tackle the content might also help. In addition, by conducting self-assessment, teachers identify areas of weakness and can then seek professional development opportunities to strengthen them. Speaking to other teachers at these courses or workshops should also give insight into new teaching strategies.

Sample Test Questions and Rationale

(Easy)

1. According to research, one of the greatest obstacles facing new teachers is which of the following:

   A. Behavioral issues

   B. Disagreements with the administration

   C. Excessive paperwork

   D. Fending off colleagues who give unwanted advice

   The answer is A.

   Research has shown that for new teachers entering the profession, the two greatest obstacles are dealing with behavioral issues and reaching students who are minimally engaged in their own learning processes.

(Average)

2. What is the most powerful benefit of teachers conducting frequent self-assessment?

   A. They identify areas of weakness and seek professional development opportunities to strengthen them

   B. By observing their own teaching, teachers save themselves the pressure of being observed by others

   C. They also learn their strengths and reduce the time spent on areas not needing attention

   D. Their practice of self-reflection offers a model for students to adopt in self-improvement

   The answer is A.

   When a teacher is involved in the process of self-reflection and self-assessment, one of the common outcomes is that the teacher comes to identify areas of skill or knowledge that require more research or improvement on his/her part. He or she may become interested in overcoming a particular weakness by attending a workshop or consulting with a mentor.

(Easy)

3. Teachers must hold themselves to high standards. When they engage in negative actions such as fighting with students, they are violating all of the following except:

   A. Ethics

   B. Professionalism

   C. Morals

   D. Fiscal

   The answer is D.

   Teachers must adhere to strict rules and regulations to maintain the highest degree of conduct and professionalism in the classroom. Current court cases in Florida have examined ethical violations of teachers engaged in improper communication and abuse with students, along with teachers engaged in drug violations and substance abuse in classrooms. It is imperative that today's teachers have the highest regard for professionalism and behave as proper role models for students in and out of the classrooms.

COMPETENCY 11
THE LARGER COMMUNITY

> **SKILL** **Knows the role of the school as a resource to the larger community**
> **11.1**

Community and Schools

In some places, the community is one entity and the school is another and rarely do the two meet. In most effective schools, community members take a lot of interest in the schools and their welfare; they constantly work to bring the two closer together. Continuing education courses are popular examples of community/school initiatives. These classes invite the community in to the building to develop interests or skills they might not be able to support otherwise.

Sports teams are another way the school becomes a part of the larger community, and in some communities the school system encourages the community to take pride and ownership in its teams. Often, blood drives and elections are held at the local school. The gyms may be the biggest meeting room in the city or county and can be utilized by the larger community.

Importance of community involvement in schools

In the early days of American public education, teachers usually lived with one of the families in the community, and the community itself felt a strong sense of ownership in the school. The feeling of ownership has lost some of its vigor as public education has become more organized, has involved political entities at higher levels, and gets more funding from local sources. Therefore, because schools are essentially owned by the people, using them as resources helps everyone. It brings the community into the school and increases a sense of ownership and community pride.

Sample Test Question and Rationale

(Average)

1. Often, schools and communities interact for the following activities except:

    A. Blood drives

    B. Legal proceedings

    C. Meeting room use

    D. Elections

The answer is B.

In some places, the community is one entity and the school is another and rarely do the two meet. Interactions may occur for blood drives and elections. In addition, because the gyms may be the biggest meeting rooms in the city or county, they can be utilized by the larger community.

SKILL 11.2 Knows factors in the students' environment outside of school *(family circumstances, community environments, health, and economic conditions)* **that may influence students' life and learning**

Outside Effects on Student Experience

Students absorb the culture and social environment around them. Often, they do so without deciphering the contextual meaning of the experiences. When provided with diverse cultural contexts, students are able to adapt and incorporate multiple meanings from cultural cues vastly different from their own. SOCIO-CULTURAL FACTORS have a definitive impact on a students' psychological, emotional, affective, and physiological development. They also affect a student's academic learning and future achievements.

> **SOCIO-CULTURAL FACTORS:** the influences of the culture and social environment around the students

A complex experience

The educational experience for most students is complicated and complex. There are diverse, interlocking meanings and inferences. If one aspect of the complexity is altered, it affects other aspects. This, in turn may impact how a student or teacher views a learning experience. Today's schools must be prepared to work with students who bring complex understandings, interpretations, and nuances. This diversity can provide many barriers to communication and learning, which, if not overcome, could impede student learning.

Physical health

In addition, health conditions affect student learning. To the extent possible, the teacher needs to know about any health issues that affect a student's performance and make accommodation for it in the classroom. Another concern is the students' food and clothing allowances. It is possible that a family is living in such poverty that the child may not have sufficient food or clothing. A teacher should call these matters to the attention of administrators and follow through to make sure the child is receiving appropriate attention.

Mental health

To learn and develop to their peak ability, students must have healthy self-images and self-worth. Students could reduce their focus on education when they are dealing with personal issues such as when they feel bullied or isolated. When a student is attending school from a homeless shelter or is lost in the middle of a parent's divorce, they are also less likely to prioritize school.

Health classes

Most schools will offer health classes that address issues including:

- Sexuality

- Self-image

- Peer pressure

- Nutrition

- Wellness

- Gang activity

- Drug engagement

- Other relevant teen experiences

In most districts, as part of a well-rounded core curriculum, students are required to take a health class. By setting this mandate, the school and district ensure that students are exposed to issues that directly affect them. In addition, by educating students in such issues, officials seek to prevent students from engaging in negative activities. Even though one health class is rarely enough to effectively address the multiplicity of such issues, in today's era of tight school budgets and financial issues, this is not likely to change.

Neglected and Abused Students

Unfortunately, many students are exposed to abuse and dangerous situations. Child abuse may manifest itself as a phenomenon known as chronic shock syndrome. The individual's nervous system becomes geared up to handle the extra flow of hormones and electrical impulses accompanying the fight or flight reaction. Each time the abuse happens, this occurs and creates a shift in the biology of the brain and allied systems. Essentially, the victim becomes allergic (hypersensitized) to stress of the kind that prevailed during the period of abuse. Recent research indicates such a shift is reflected in brain chemistry and structural changes and may last a lifetime.

Abused vs. neglected

The abused student differs from the neglected one. While the neglected student suffers from understimulation, the abused one suffers from overstimulation. The neglected student will be:

- Withdrawn

- Quiet

- Almost sedate

In contrast, the abused student may be:

- Angry

- Energetic

- Rebellious

- Aggressive

- Hard to control

In each case, the environment of abuse or neglect shapes the behavior of the student away from home. Often, out of reflex, the student will flinch when seeming to anticipate a blow, or may be unable to accept or understand healthy attention directed to him or her. To sense what the student's feelings and experiences may be, the teacher merely needs to watch the student's reaction to a loud noise, someone's aggression, or the response when offered some companionship by another youth.

Signs of physical abuse

Obvious signs of physical abuse are marks from:

- Hand

- Fist

- Belt

- Coat hanger

- Kitchen utensil

- Extension cord

- Any other imaginable implement for striking and inflicting pain

To effectively help the child, the suspicion has to be backed up with hard evidence. Unusual marks in geometric shapes may indicate the presence of an implement for spanking such as a spoon, homemade paddle, extension cord, or coat hanger. Marks on the arms and legs may indicate being whipped there. Teachers should always be suspicious about bruises.

Evaluating injuries

Bruises on the neck and face usually do not come from a student tripping and falling. Rather, they are usually the result of intentional hitting—and even choking. Noting the sizes and shapes of bruises and using simple imagination may reveal the source of the injury. The observer should notice whether the bruise has reddened areas, indicating ruptured capillaries, or is uniformly colored but shaded a darker color toward the perimeter. The rupture of capillaries indicates a strong hit, while the shaded bruise indicates a softer compression.

The educator who discovers any of these conditions should start with a reasonable suspicion that abuse is occuring. They would then gather specific indicators and firm evidence, not only for the sake of the child, but also when the report is scruitinized. Take note of the size of the injury, and describe it in concrete terms. For instance, describe a bruise as being the size of a quarter or an orange.

Signs of neglect

When identifying the neglected student, teachers can look for signs of malnourishment. For instance, a student may gorge at lunch, yet still be thin and underweight. This student may be quiet and shy, shabbily groomed, and unconcerned about his or her appearance. Poor nutrition at home may result in an unusually high number of colds. It is of utmost importance to guarantee that immunizations are current, as they probably have been overlooked. Students who are neglected are usually not very social, may isolate themselves, and may not respond to invitations to join other youth in activities. These are not necessarily signs of neglect since any student can display these traits from time to time. However, if they are accompanied by a persistant social anxiety, this may indicate that something is happening at home.

Signs of sexual abuse

In cases of sexual abuse the most blatant warning sign is the oversexualization by the student. They become interested in sexually related matters long before their developmental stage would predict. They may be seen to quietly masturbate at prepubescent ages and may even act out sexually with other children of their own age. If a student suddenly begins to engage in promiscuous sexual behavior, this is a sign that he or she is being molested. Sexual abuse of children is widespread and takes many forms. Kissing episodes by a parent or other adult, when out of normal context, are just as damaging as more overt forms of contact. The sexualized leer or stare by a perverted parent or adult can also be damaging. Deal with all situations of sexual abuse with extreme care. It is advised to wait for the trained professional who knows the methodology. Incorrectly conducted information gathering can be detrimental to a prosecution.

A Successful Environment

The student's capacity and potential for academic success is a product of his or her ability and the total environment, which is composed of the classroom and school system, home and family, and neighborhood and community. All of these segments are interrelated and can be supportive, one of the other, or divisive, one against the other. As a matter of course, the teacher will become familiar with all aspects of the system, the school, and the classroom. This would include not only processes and protocols but also the availability of resources provided to meet the academic, health, and welfare needs of students. But it is incumbent upon the teacher to look beyond the boundaries of the school system to identify additional resources as well as issues and situations that will effect (directly or indirectly) a student's ability to succeed in the classroom.

Resources for success

Initial contacts for resources outside of the school system will usually come from within the system itself, from administration, teacher organizations, department heads, and other colleagues. Resources can include libraries, museums, zoos, planetariums, etc. Teachers can obtain materials, media, speakers, and presenters from:

- Nonprofit organizations
- Social clubs
- Societies
- Civic organizations
- Community outreach programs of private businesses, corporations, and governmental agencies

Departments of social services can provide background and program information relevant to social issues, which may be impacting individual students. In turn, this can be a resource for classroom instruction regarding life skills, at-risk behaviors, and related areas.

Sample Test Question and Rationale

(Rigorous)

1. **Which of these is not a reason why schools offer health classes that address issues of sexuality, self-image, peer pressure, nutrition, wellness, gang activity, and drug engagement?**

   A. In order to establish a core curriculum that is well-rounded

   B. Because health education is mandated by Title X

   C. To prevent students from engaging in negative activities

   D. So that students are exposed to issues that directly affect them

The answer is B.

Most schools will offer health classes that address issues of sexuality, self-image, peer pressure, nutrition, wellness, gang activity, drug engagement, and a variety of other relevant teen experiences. In most districts, as part of a well-rounded core-curriculum, students are required to take a health class. By setting this mandate, the school and district ensure that students are exposed to issues that directly affect them. In addition, by educating students in such issues, officials seek to prevent students from engaging in negative activities. Even though one health class is rarely enough to effectively address the multiplicity of such issues, in today's era of tight school budgets and financial issues, this is not likely to change.

> ### SKILL 11.3 Develops and utilizes active partnerships among teachers, parents/guardians, and leaders in the community to support the educational process

Support System for Teachers

The teacher is the manager of his or her classroom. This can seem a lonely business, especially when there is a particularly troubled or troubling student or group of students. In reality, teachers are never alone, they have colleagues who are usually more than willing to step in and help. Sharing ownership of the classroom with other teachers makes the job tenable, particularly if the other teachers may be dealing with the same students,. They can, together, develop an effective strategy. The same is true of parents. That relationship must not be adversarial unless there is no other way to handle the student and the situation.

Developing partnerships

In communications with other teachers, administration, and parents, respectful, reciprocal communication solves many problems. This is especially true if the teacher truly respects the opinions and ideas of others involved in the life of the students. The teacher may be the classroom expert, but parents are usually well versed on what is going on with their child. Bringing them into the decision-making process may lead to solutions and success beyond what the teacher could envision. The teacher may be in the life of the student for a few hours each day, five days a week, nine months of the year, but the parents' role in the life of their child is constant. A sense of partnership between parents and teacher is vital and useful. When decisions are made regarding the management of the student in the classroom, the decisions should be shared.

> ### SKILL 11.4 Knows major laws related to students' rights and teacher responsibilities *(need equal education, appropriate education for students' with special needs, confidentiality and privacy, appropriate treatment of students)*

Americans with Disabilities Act

AMERICANS WITH DISABILITIES ACT: federal law passed in 1990 designed to prevent discrimination against students with disabilities

The school system also offers resources for teachers to help their students. All schools have guidelines for receiving this assistance especially since the implementation of the **AMERICANS WITH DISABILITIES ACT**. The first step in securing help is for the teacher to approach the school's administration or exceptional education department. These offices will provide direction in obtaining special services or resources for qualifying students. As discussed in section 2.3, many schools have a committee designated for addressing these needs such as a Child Study or Core Team (CST). These teams are made up of both regular and exceptional education teachers, school psychologists, guidance counselors, and administrators.

The classroom teacher usually has to complete initial paperwork and conduct behavioral observations. This information then goes to the appropriate committee for discussion and consideration. Next, the committee recommends the course of action to be taken. Often subsequent steps include a complete psychological evaluation, certain physical examinations such as vision and hearing screening tests, and a complete medical examination by a doctor. Usually it is relatively simple for the classroom teacher to refer students and may only require initial paperwork and discussion. The services and resources the student receives as a result of the process typically prove to be invaluable.

Needs beyond the school

At times, the teacher must go beyond the school system to meet the needs of some students. An awareness of special services and resources and how to obtain them is essential. When the school system is unable to address the needs of a student, the teacher must often take the initiative and contact agencies within the community. Frequently there is no special policy for finding resources. It is up to the individual teacher to be creative and resourceful and to find whatever help the student needs. Meeting the needs of all students is certainly a team effort that is most often spearheaded by the classroom teacher.

At times, the teacher must go beyond the school system to meet the needs of some students. An awareness of special services and resources and how to obtain them is essential.

Equal Education
TITLE 20—EDUCATION, CHAPTER 39—EQUAL EDUCATIONAL OPPORTUNITIES, SUBCHAPTER I—EQUAL EDUCATIONAL OPPORTUNITIES Part 2—Unlawful Practices.

Americans with Disabilities Act of 1990: Title II Regulations
Amendments to regulations governing nondiscrimination on the basis of disability in local and state government services.

Section 504 of the Rehabilitation Act of 1973 Regulations
Amendments to regulations governing nondiscrimination on the basis of disability in education or activities receiving federal financial assistance.

Title IX of the Education Amendments of 1972 Regulations
Amendments to regulations governing nondiscrimination on the basis of sex in education or activities receiving federal financial assistance.

Title VI of the Civil Rights Act of 1964 Regulations
Amendments to regulations governing nondiscrimination of programs receiving Department of Education funding.

Appropriate Education for Students
See Skill 1.1

Appropriate Treatment of Students

Federal laws

Title IX of the Education Amendments of 1972 does not mention sexual harassment but, rather, is a statute that prohibits discrimination on the basis of sex in any educational organization that receives federal funds.[1] Title IX provides for federal enforcement of this prohibition and violating institutions face the possibility of losing their federal funds.

Twenty years after the enactment of Title IX, the Supreme Court in *Franklin v. Gwinnett County Public Schools*, 503 U.S. 60 (1992) ruled that students may seek monetary damages from schools for sexual harassment visited on them by school employees. This ruling was groundbreaking because it equated sexual harassment in schools with sexual discrimination and it assigned schools monetary liability for damages. Franklin did not, however, provide educators a clear framework for understanding their legal responsibilities to provide a school environment that was free from harassment.

The Office for Civil Rights (OCR) enforces Title IX and its regulations and publishes guidelines to help schools recognize and effectively respond to sexual harassment of students in educational programs. As a condition of receiving federal financial-assistance, schools must avail themselves of this resource when necessary. OCR also provides technical assistance to schools in developing sexual harassment policies to clarify the responsibilities of school personnel. Schools are responsible for prohibiting and responding effectively to sexual harassment and there are potential legal consequences for ignoring sexual harassment of students by staff or other students.

---

[1] Title IX states that "No person in the United States shall, on the basis of sex, be excluded from participation in, be denied the benefits of, or be subjected to discrimination under any education program or activity receiving Federal financial assistance" (Title IX, Section 1681).

SUGGESTIONS AND RECOMMENDATIONS FROM THE LITERATURE FOR POSSIBLE LEGISLATION AND REGULATIONS	
Liability	Under Title IX, school districts shall be held liable for damages for a teacher's sexual harassment of a student based upon the same guidelines as Title VII.
Prohibition	No person in a position of trust may engage in sexual conduct with students 18 years old and younger, regardless of any state's age of consent. Violation is considered a Class C felony. There are no confidential settlements with alleged abusers; there is no discretion for judges in imposing settlements.
Reporting	Violators of the federal law would be required to register as sex offenders. Mandated reporting of conviction by adjudicating agency and by educators; failure to report would be a gross misdemeanor and result in the forfeiture of one's professional education license. Required reporting to the state licensing agency of all allegations of educator sexual misconduct, including those that result in a termination or resignation. State data collection and reporting on extent of educator sexual misconduct. National clearinghouse on educator sexual misconduct.
Requirement	There is a 10-year statute of limitations on filing complaints and bringing charges. Mandatory background, fingerprinting, and interim employment career checks are required for all teachers and school employees (not only those who are newly hired). School officials must ask former employees whether a job applicant had a history of sexual misconduct or allegations of such.

Privacy and Confidentiality

THE PRIVACY ACT OF 1974 5 U.S.C. § 552a:

http://www.usdoj.gov/foia/privstat.htm

SAMPLE TEST

(Average) (Skill 5.1)

1. **What would improve planning for instruction?**

   A. Describing the role of the teacher and student

   B. Assessing the outcomes of prior instruction

   C. Rearranging the order of activities

   D. Giving outside assignments

(Rigorous) (Skill 6.1)

2. **Of the following definitions, which best describes a standardized achievement test?**

   A. It measures narrow skills and abilities

   B. It measures broad areas of knowledge

   C. It measures the ability to perform a task

   D. It measures performance related to specific, recently acquired information

(Rigorous) (Skill 6.1)

3. **Norm-referenced tests:**

   A. Provide information about how local test takers performed compared to local test takers from the previous year

   B. Provide information about how the local test takers performed compared to a representative sampling of national test takers

   C. Make no comparisons to national test takers

   D. None of the above

(Rigorous) (Skill 2.4)

4. **When students provide evidence of having special needs, standardized tests can be:**

   A. Given out with the same predetermined questions as what is administered to students without special needs

   B. Exempted for students children whose special-needs conditions would prevent them performing with any reliability or validity

   C. Administered over a lengthier test period (i.e., four hours instead of three or two)

   D. All of the above

(Rigorous) (Skill 6.2)

5. **Which of the following is the least appropriate reason for teachers to be able to analyze data on their students?**

   A. To provide appropriate instruction

   B. To make instructional decisions

   C. To separate students into weaker and stronger academic groups

   D. To communicate and determine instructional progress

(Average) (Skill 6.1)

6. **It is most appropriate to use norm-referenced standardized tests for which of the following?**

   A. For comparison to the population on which the test was normed

   B. For teacher evaluation

   C. For evaluation of the administration

   D. For comparison to school on which the test was normed

(Easy) (Skill 1.1)

7. Constructivist classrooms are considered to be:

    A. Student-centered

    B. Teacher-centered

    C. Focused on standardized tests

    D. Requiring little creativity

(Average) (Skill 1.1)

8. Which of the following is not a stage in Piaget's theory of child development?

    A. Sensory motor stage

    B. Preoptimal stage

    C. Concrete operational

    D. Formal operational

(Rigorous) (Skill 2.1)

9. Mr. Rogers describes his educational philosophy as eclectic, meaning that he uses many educational theories to guide his classroom practice. Why is this the best approach for today's teachers?

    A. Today's classrooms are often too diverse for one theory to meet the needs of all students

    B. Educators must be able to draw upon other strategies if one theory is not effective

    C. Both A and B

    D. None of the above

(Rigorous) (Skill 3.2)

10. Mrs. Grant is providing her students with many extrinsic motivators in order to increase their intrinsic motivation. Which of the following best explains this relationship?

    A. This is a good relationship and will increase intrinsic motivation

    B. The relationship builds animosity between the teacher and the students

    C. Extrinsic motivation does not in itself help to build intrinsic motivation

    D. There is no place for extrinsic motivation in the classroom

(Average) (Skill 2.2)

11. This condition has skyrocketed among young children, usually presents itself within the first three years of a child's life, and hinders normal communication and social interactive behavior.

    A. ADHD

    B. Dyslexia

    C. Depression

    D. Autism

(Easy) (Skill 6.1)

12. Which of the following test items is not objective?

    A. Multiple choice

    B. Essay

    C. Matching

    D. True/false

(Easy) (Skill 2.5)

13. **What is one of the most important things to know about the differences between first language (L1) and second language (L2) acquisition?**

    A. A second language is easier to acquire than a first language

    B. Most people master a second language (L2) , but rarely do they master a first language (L1)

    C. Most people master a first language (L1), but rarely do they master a second language (L2)

    D. Acquiring a first language (L1) takes the same level of difficulty as acquiring a second language (L2)

(Easy) (Skill 3.3)

14. **A teacher's posture and movement affect the following student outcomes except:**

    A. Student learning

    B. Attitudes

    C. Motivation

    D. Physical development

(Average) (Skill 3.4)

15. **Which statement is an example of specific individual praise?**

    A. "John, you are the only person in class not paying attention."

    B. "William, I thought we agreed that you would turn in all of your homework."

    C. "Robert, you did a good job staying in line. See how it helped us get to music class on time."

    D. "Class, you did a great job cleaning up the art room."

(Easy) (Skill 4.1)

16. **What is the most important benefit of students developing critical thinking skills?**

    A. Students are able to apply knowledge to a specific subject area as well as other subject areas

    B. Students remember the information for testing purposes

    C. Students focus on a limited number of specific facts

    D. Students do not have to memorize the information for later recall

(Average) (Skill 4.2)

17. **Learning centers are unique instructional tools because they allow students to do all of the following except?**

    A. Learn through play

    B. Sit in their seats to complete assignments

    C. Select their own activities

    D. Set up the activity area under a teacher's guidance

(Average) (Skill 4.4)

18. **Describe the difference between a LAN and a WAN?**

    A. WANs allow computers to communicate over greater distances than LANs

    B. LANs allow computers to communicate over greater distances than WANs

    C. WANs and LANs provide the same geographical range

    D. WANs and LANs are both ineffective

(Rigorous) (Skill 5.1)

19. **Teachers must use lesson plans to do all of the following except:**

    A. Meet specified goals and objectives

    B. Match the lesson to students' abilities and needs

    C. Test a strategy proposed by a research journal

    D. Meet state and local learning standards

(Rigorous) (Skill 5.2)

20. **Two powerful internal factors influencing students' academic focus and success are their _____ and _____.**

    A. resources and class sizes

    B. parental involvement and teacher preparation

    C. efforts and academic outcomes

    D. attitudes and perceptions about learning

(Easy) (Skill 6.2)

21. **The seven purposes of assessment, include all of the following except:**

    A. To identify students' strengths and weaknesses

    B. To assess the effectiveness of a particular instructional strategy

    C. To provide data that assists in decision making

    D. None of the above

(Average) (Skill 6.2)

22. **What is the best example of a formative assessment?**

    A. The results of an intelligence test

    B. Correcting tests in small groups and immediately recording the grades

    C. An essay that receives teacher feedback and can be corrected by students prior to having a grade recorded

    D. Scheduling a discussion prior to the test

(Rigorous) (Skill 6.3)

23. **Fill in the blanks for I. _____ and II. _____ in the picture below:**

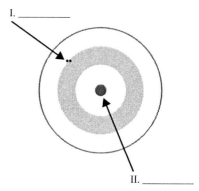

    A. I. Reliability and II. Validity

    B. I. Validity and II. Reliability

    C. I. Reliability and II. Vigor

    D. I. Rigor and II. Validity

(Easy) (Skill 7.1)

24. **Outlines, graphs, and models are particularly good for which type of learners?**

    A. Auditory

    B. Kinestetic

    C. Visual

    D. Olfactory

(Average) (Skill 8.1)

25. To facilitate discussion-oriented, nonthreatening communication among all students, teachers must do which of the following:

    A. Model appropriate behavior

    B. Allow students to express themselves freely

    C. Show students that some views will not be tolerated

    D. Explain that students should not disagree

(Rigorous) (Skill 9.1)

26. Which of the following is the best strategy to probe for student understanding of a specific topic?

    A. Assigning writing exercises that are graded for correctness

    B. Allowing students to write on any topic

    C. C. Suggesting that students write in a journal that is checked at the end of the semester

    D. Assigning writing exercises that focus on recording students' thoughts on the topic

(Average) (Skill 10.1)

27. Teachers should network with one another for all of the following reasons except _____.

    A. to discuss challenges they face in their classrooms

    B. to develop a sense of community

    C. to earn their clock-hours for licensure renewal

    D. to find solutions to difficult problems

(Rigorous) (Skill 10.2)

28. Ms. Jones has just read an article on an exciting new instructional strategy; she is considering incorporating this strategy in her classroom. As a research-oriented professional, what should be her next step?

    A. Read textbooks that deal with a wide range of theories

    B. Perform a literature search to see what else has been written on the topic

    C. Talk with other teachers about their opinions

    D. Begin incorporating the strategy with some students in the class

(Easy) (Skill 10.3)

29. According to research, one of the greatest obstacles facing new teachers is which of the following?

    A. Behavioral issues

    B. Disagreements with the administration

    C. Excessive paperwork

    D. Fending off colleagues who give unwanted advice

(Average) (Skill 11.1)

30. Often, schools and communities interact for the following activities except:

    A. Blood drives

    B. Legal proceedings

    C. Meeting room use

    D. Elections

(Rigorous) (Skill 4.2)

31. Discovery learning is to inquiry as direct instruction is to...

    A. Loosely developed lessons

    B. Clear instructions

    C. Random lessons

    D. Class discussion

(Rigorous) (Skill 3.4)

32. In the classroom, the concept of management transition describes:

    A. How the administration switches between the principal and vice principal

    B. How parents are prepared for when their children move from one grade to the next

    C. How students monitor the time they spend moving from class to class

    D. How teachers use time effectively so the class moves smoothly from one activity to another

(Average) (Skill 4.1)

33. How can mnemonic devices be used to increase achievement?

    A. They help students learn to pronounce assigned terms

    B. They provide visual cues to help students recall information

    C. They give auditory hints to increase learner retention

    D. They are most effective with kinesthetic learners

(Easy) (Skill 6.3)

34. This method tests the validity and reliability of a test by dividing a single test into two parts and comparing them.

    A. Split-half

    B. Test-retest

    C. Equivalent forms

    D. Two-set

(Average) (Skill 7.1)

35. What has research shown to be the effect of using advance organizers in the lesson?

    A. They facilitate learning and retention

    B. They allow teachers to use their planning time effectively

    C. They only serve to help the teacher organize the lesson

    D. They show definitive positive results on student achievement

(Average) (Skill 10.3)

36. What is the most powerful benefit of teachers conducting frequent self-assessment?

    A. They identify areas of weakness and seek professional development opportunities to strengthen them

    B. By observing their own teaching, teachers save themselves the pressure of being observed by others

    C. They also learn their strengths and reduce the time spent on areas not needing attention

    D. Their practice of self-reflection offers a model for students to adopt in self-improvement

(Average) (Skill 2.2)

37. The difference between typical stress-response behavior and severe emotional distress can be identified by the:

    A. Situation, circumstances, and individuals around which the behavior occurs

    B. The family dynamics of the student

    C. Frequency, duration, and intensity of the stress-responsive behavior

    D. The student's age, maturity, and coping abilities

(Easy) (Skill 2.2)

38. It is essential that teachers develop relationships with their students and are aware of their personalities. Which of the following is an example of why this is important?

    A. Because most students do not have adult friends

    B. Because most teachers do not have friends who are students

    C. So that teachers can stay abreast of the social interaction between students

    D. Because then teachers can immediately identify behavioral changes and get the student help

(Easy) (Skill 2.3)

39. Which of the following does the least to address the needs of students with disabilities?

    A. IDEA

    B. Title IX

    C. P.L. 94-142

    D. Least restrictive environment

(Easy) (Skill 4.2)

40. This instructional strategy engages students in active discussion about issues and problems of practical application.

    A. Case method

    B. Direct instruction

    C. Concept mapping

    D. Formative assessment

(Average) (Skill 8.1)

41. In diverse classrooms, teachers must ensure that they neither protect students from criticism nor praise them because of their ethnicity or gender. Doing either action may result in which of the following outcomes?

    A. Classmates may become anxious or resentful when dealing with the diverse students

    B. Parents will appreciate their child being singled out

    C. The student will be pleased to receive this attention

    D. Other teachers will follow this example

(Easy) (Skill 10.3)

42. Teachers must hold themselves to high standards. When they engage in negative actions such as fighting with students, they are violating all of the following except:

    A. Ethics

    B. Professionalism

    C. Morals

    D. Fiscal

(Rigorous) (Skill 2.1)

43. Which of the following statements MOST explains how philosophy has impacted other subject areas such as reading, math, and science?

    A. Most subject areas emerged from Greek society and its great philosophers such as Plato and Aristotle

    B. Using philosophical arguments, experts have debated the best teaching strategies in various subject areas

    C. Philosophy drives the motivation and dedication of most great teachers

    D. A majority of the fifty states require students to take several years of philosophical courses

(Easy) (Skill 3.4)

44. A laminated seating chart can assist teachers in simplifying all of the following tasks except:

    A. Performing self-assessments

    B. Taking attendance

    C. Making daily notes

    D. Keeping track of participation

(Average) (Skill 2.1)

45. You notice that one of your students is having a seizure and classmates inform you that this is because she was abusing drugs at her locker. What should you do immediately after contacting the main office about this emergency?

    A. Attempt to treat the student

    B. Find out the protocol for your school district

    C. Isolate the student until EMS or police arrive

    D. Interview classmates individually to gather the facts

(Rigorous) (Skill 11.2)

46. Which of these is not a reason why schools offer health classes that address issues of sexuality, self-image, peer pressure, nutrition, wellness, gang activity, and drug engagement?

    A. In order to establish a core curriculum that is well-rounded

    B. Because health education is mandated by Title X

    C. To prevent students from engaging in negative activities

    D. So that students are exposed to issues that directly affect them

(Easy) (Skill 4.4)

47. A computer network includes physical infrastructure such as which of the following?

    A. Software

    B. Web sites

    C. Operating systems

    D. Cables

(Average) (Skill 6.3)

48. An example of reliability in testing is:

    A. Items on the test produce the same response each time

    B. The test was administered with poor lighting

    C. Items on the test measure what they should measure

    D. The test is too long for the time allotted

(Rigorous) (Skill 6.1)

49. _____ is a standardized test in which performance is directly related to the educational objective(s).

    A. Aptitude test

    B. Norm-referenced test

    C. Criterion-referenced test

    D. Summative evaluation

(Average) (Skill 2.3)

50. Free appropriate education, the individual education program, procedural safeguards, and least restrictive environment; identify the legislation represented by these elements.

    A. Americans with Disabilities Act

    B. The Equal Access Act

    C. The Individuals with Disabilities Education Act

    D. Title VI, The Civil Rights Act of 1964

ANSWER KEY

1. B	7. A	13. C	19. C	25. A	31. B	37. A	43. B	49. C
2. B	8. B	14. D	20. D	26. D	32. D	38. D	44. A	50. C
3. B	9. C	15. C	21. D	27. C	33. B	39. B	45. C	
4. D	10. C	16. A	22. C	28. B	34. A	40. C	46. B	
5. C	11. D	17. B	23. A	29. A	35. A	41. A	47. D	
6. A	12. B	18. A	24. C	30. B	36. A	42. D	48. A	

RIGOR TABLE

Rigor level	Questions
Easy 20%	7, 12, 13, 14, 16, 21, 24, 29, 34, 38, 39, 40, 42, 44, 47
Average Rigor 40%	1, 6, 8, 11, 15, 17, 18, 22, 25, 27, 30, 33, 35, 36, 37, 41, 45, 48, 50
Rigorous 40%	2, 3, 4, 5, 9, 10, 19, 20, 23, 26, 28, 31, 32, 35, 43, 46, 49

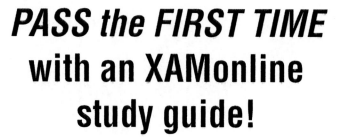